ANGELS

Demons

and **other**
flying creatures

From the Bible–Teaching Ministry of
Stephen Davey

Angels, Demons, and Other Flying Creatures

Author: Stephen Davey
Editorial Team: Lalanne Barber, J. Seth Davey, Marsha Davey
Cover Design and Body Layout: Grace Gourley
Photo of Stephen: Sam Gray Portraits, Raleigh, NC (samgrayportraits.com)

Unless otherwise noted, all Scripture quotations are from the New American Standard Bible®, Copyright © 1960, 1962, 1963, 1968, 1971, 1972, 1973, 1975, 1995 by the Lockman Foundation. Used by permission.

Consideration has been made to footnote sources whenever necessary. In the case of any unintentional omission, future editions will include appropriate notations.

Contents

Angelmania

Those Elusive Flying Creatures

There is no doubt that the subject of the spirit world has produced unbelievable fascination and an entire industry of speculation. People everywhere are fascinated with the existence and role of **angels** and **demons**. Today more people are talking about heaven, angels, and the spirit world than ever before.

Now you may wonder who the other **flying creatures** are, so let's start with a brief discussion of them.

There are **cherubim** and **seraphim** that fly about doing the bidding of our sovereign God. They may simply be hovering around His throne at this very moment chanting, "Holy, holy, holy."

There are also the **spirits of deceased believers** who have, so to speak, flown to heaven and are capable, even now, of transcending space.

There will be the **future glorified bodies of believers** who, like Christ, will be able to materialize and dematerialize at will. Jesus Christ walked through a closed door and yet ate fish. Believers will also be able to be in one place and then fly to another point in the blink of an eye. Those of us who have trusted in Christ will be able to travel without needing to walk between the new heaven and the new earth, while enjoying the eternal service and worship of God, as the book of Revelation reveals.

So, introduce yourself to others by saying, "Hello, I'm one of God's future flying creatures!"

Obsessed with Angels

Beliefs outside the Church

Well over a hundred books are currently in print on the subject of angels and the afterlife. Not too long ago, five of the top ten books on a list of religious bestsellers were books dealing with the subject of angels.

One book that topped the charts for many months was a how-to guide instructing people on methods of contacting angels, communicating with them, and even receiving guidance from them.

A well-known publisher lists these titles in its catalogue:

- *Angel Letters*
- *Angel Power*
- *Angel's Bidding*
- *Angels and Aliens*
- *The Angels Weep*
- *Angels over Their Shoulder*
- *The Angels within Us*
- *Ask Your Angel*
- *An Angel to Watch over Me*

And this list only includes the listings under the letter "A"!

Television specials and network programs such as *Touched by an Angel, Highway to Heaven, Angels: the Mysterious Messengers,* and *Angels: Beyond the Light* have communicated fiction about angels that has become, more or less, gospel truth.

According to a survey reported in *Time Magazine*, sixty-nine percent of those participating believed in the existence of angels, and forty-six percent believed they had a guardian angel. My wife believes I have a guardian angel that rides around on the front bumper of my F-150!

There is an angel-watch network in New Jersey that exists to monitor angelic comings and goings. They have a bimonthly journal with thousands of subscribers.

The Angel Collectors Club of America has members who exchange everything from angel cookie jars to angel food recipes. They hold a national convention every two years. Seminars on angels are packing rooms in cities and filling rural retreats.

Angelmania is in full swing. If you had talked about the existence of angels to average people on the street thirty years ago, they would have thought you a little off in the head. Today, however, if you suggest that spirit beings do not exist or that they have no interplay with human beings, you would be considered out of touch and close-minded.

Books, seminars, CDs, and pamphlets (now considered mainstream) promise the following:

- Through the easy techniques presented in this book, you can learn to access and attune to beings such as guardian angels, nature spirits, and archangels.
- Everyone has a Spirit Guide or guardian angel who assists him in

keeping on a chosen path. This CD helps you get in touch with yours.

- This book enables you to begin to open your heart to these joyful and comforting protectors, so you can raise your consciousness to a new dimension.

- You can learn, through the use of a combination of your birth sign and a specific colored candle how to obtain the magic and wisdom you want in life by calling upon the angels. This book contains many spiritual secrets that will guide the reader to success and power.

- This book will teach nine specific ways your personal angel protects you, how to call out to your guardian angel, and how to get your angel to answer your cry for help and assistance in matters big and small. You will also find out about the angelic hierarchy and learn the actual language of the angelic kingdom.

Much of this, as one author commented, is little more than occult divination, sorcery, and New Age mysticism.

Protestant Beliefs about Angels

If you ask the average Protestant about angels, you will get a mixed bag of answers. Major denominational leaders are currently debating the eternality of hell and the future existence of spirits. Many actually deny the literal personality of Satan and say instead that he is simply a metaphor for all that is evil—he really does not exist.

Others within the more evangelical realm have been caught up in a form of animism. This is the belief in the existence of individual spirits that inhabit natural objects and phenomena.

Neil Anderson, a popular evangelical author, has gone so far as to say that the evil spirits can be unknowingly passed through generations. He encouraged people not to adopt children unless they could be present at the time of birth and bind the evil spirit with a special prayer.

Believers are focusing on binding spirit beings that hold territories under their sway. It is not unusual any more to hear that the strategies of classic evangelism and intentional missions are being set aside in favor of simply praying down/out the demons that bind a particular neighborhood, city, state, or country.

Catholic Beliefs about Angels

On the other side of the Reformation line, Roman Catholicism has a confusing history regarding angels and demons.

Several of the more recent popes have encouraged prayer to guardian angels. Pope John addressed one group and said, "We particularly ask our guardian angel to help us in our daily ministry."

Former monks and scholars such as Francis Borgia and Bernard of Clairvaux encouraged devotion and prayer to angels. The new Catechism of the Catholic Church includes the words "From infancy to death, human life is surrounded by their watchful care and intercession. Beside each believer stands an angel as protector and shepherd, leading him to life."

I suppose, if this is true, then David got it wrong and should have written in verse one of the Twenty-Third Psalm, "The guardian angel is my shepherd, I shall not want."

Now understand, my purpose is not to offend just Catholics and mainline Protestants here but, rather, to offend *everyone*. It is my desire to trouble and provoke *everyone* into critically thinking that we should take the **Bible alone** as the authority for faith and practice.

I believe it's a spiritual jungle out there. If all we do is listen to the latest stories and get caught up in the latest fads, we will get lost in that jungle and become disoriented about our Christian walk and our spiritual heritage.

It's interesting to me that Scripture gives believers two very strong warnings that are specifically related to **angels** and **demons**. Paul writes these warnings:

> *I am amazed that you are so quickly deserting Him who called you by the grace of Christ, for a different gospel; which is really not another; only there are some who are disturbing you and want to distort the gospel of Christ. But even if we, or an angel from heaven, should preach to you a gospel contrary to what we have preached to you, he is to be accursed* (Galatians 1:6-8)*!*

> **[E]*ven Satan disguises himself as an angel of light*** (2 Corinthians 11:14)**.**

Of course he does! Satan is darkness, not light; he *disguises* himself as *spiritual enlightenment.* He is not truth; he is the father of lies and disguises his lies with kernels of truth.

How many people would be fooled or tempted to follow Satan if he showed up wearing a red suit, carrying a pitchfork, and had a long, pointed tail and horns? Yet, how many people have been fooled by those who claim to have seen some figure or form or vision of light and assumed it must be from God?

Paul warned Pastor Timothy:

But the Spirit explicitly says that in later times some will fall away from the faith, paying attention to deceitful spirits and doctrines of demons (1 Timothy 4:1)**.**

If there was ever a need for biblical investigation, it is today. The believer needs to **know** the truth about the spirit world, as well as have a biblical perspective about that unseen universe.

In our study throughout this series, I will answer two questions:

1. Why is there so much interest in the spirit world?
2. What is it about angels and the spirit world that is so alluring and fascinating to society at large?

A New Source of Additional Wisdom?

Perhaps one answer to the previous questions is a belief that angels provide a new source of supernatural wisdom.

This is not really new—it is just continually repackaged deception. It may come in the form of the angel Moroni appearing to Joseph Smith with supposedly "new" revelations about God, or it may come from first-century mystics called Gnostics who believed they had special *gnosis* (knowledge) from God.

The Gnostics even produced secret books that gave initiates the names of demons and the names of the angels who could combat those demons. Rituals, magic, and taboo were the keys to the door of enlightenment, and angels appeared to be the guides, teachers, and friends.

The Apostle Paul would call this the myths and doctrines of demons.

There is a woman near Calgary, Alberta, who claims to have a remarkable gift. She says if you tell her your full name, she can go into meditation, focus on a candle, and have a vision of your guardian angel.

She will get a message (which is usually a few pages long) for you from the angel and will also sketch a picture of the angel, all yours to keep. You thus get to find out what your guardian angel looks like and have a direct word of wisdom from him as well. The woman charges two hundred dollars per vision.

One author writes,

What could be more comforting in an age of broken families, economic uncertainty, rising crime, and loss of personal worth? "Love yourself unconditionally, because we love you and we are always with you," our angels tell us. Angels make no demands except that we accept ourselves; they take us nowhere but to the path of greater strength and self-fulfillment, and they predict nothing for our planet except the dawn of a new age of understanding and spirituality. What is there not to like? How could it possibly hurt to have a picture of your angel as a reminder of your spiritual friend?

In the mean time, don't worry about doctrinal issues or fret over inconsistencies with the Gospel of Christ in the messages they deliver.

If you read the materials, you will discover that the angels do not care whether you are Jewish, Muslim, Mormon, Christian, Hindu, or Native American. In fact they will quote from the Bible, the *Book of Mormon*, the *Quran*, and/or the *Tanakh*.

The angels are here to help us manage life and planet Earth.

In the best seller *Ask Your Angels*, Earth itself is considered empowered by an angel named Gaia. She is referred to as "Earth Angel," which is not to be confused with that musical golden oldie "Earth Angel." No, this version teaches us about nature spirits and the noble intelligence of trees; the angels will give wisdom to mankind so it can put the earth in order.

The truth is, none of this is new wisdom; it is old **mythology**.

You can, for example, go back centuries to the time when *The Books of Enoch* were bestsellers. Mystics, over the course of the third and fourth centuries, compiled them in their belief that Enoch of the Old Testament had a special relationship with the angels. This resulted in chronicling a series of startling events. When Enoch was taken up to heaven, he passed through ten heavens and observed various angels going about their duties. He saw the two hundred angels who govern the stars, as well those who kept the treasuries of snow and ice. He also witnessed the 150,000 who accompany the sun in its trek across the sky and the weird flying spirits that dwell in its path. Eventually Enoch reached the tenth heaven where he was taken into the presence of God. Then the angel Vrevoil came and taught Enoch in all things for thirty days and thirty nights. Enoch was capable of not only listening but of writing it all down to produce 366 books. These books are supposed sources of new wisdom in addition to Scripture.

One book on angels claims to be a "primer for learning how to talk to celestials" and purports to become a "textbook for your life."

So the "new" wisdom of the twenty-first century is not new—it is old fantasy dressed in different clothes. The unsuspecting person who is intrigued by angels is often pulled into a web of delusion, occultism, and speculation, in which the Bible is set aside in favor of *new* wisdom . . . a *new* gospel . . . a *new* path.

A New Promise of Additional Assistance?

Angels are fascinating to the human mind and heart because of the belief that they provide a new promise of additional assistance.

This is, again, not new. Praying to angels for assistance became so rampant within the Church during the fourth century that the Council of Laodicea passed a resolution forbidding anyone to pray to angels.

Today, angels are credited with all sorts of miraculous interventions, and even emotions.

One author gushes, "If you are feeling joy, you are feeling the angels."

There are angels for every occasion, including healers, worry extinguishers, and prosperity brokers. And if you can't find the kind of angel you want on the list, no need to worry—there are **designer angels** who can help with almost any task you assign. Some angels specialize in education. When you suddenly have a good idea, I hope you are not so vain as to suppose that you actually thought of it yourself. Not at all—an angel gave it to you!

This is paganism with a pretty face on it. Pagan religions believed that everything had a god associated with it. There were gods of famine, luck, war, disease, good crops, protection, conception, child birth, death, and other occurrences!

The **angelmania** of today has merely exchanged gods for angels and demons.

As paganism infiltrates the Church, there is the corresponding belief that while all that is good has an angel to thank, whatever is bad or sinful is the work of demons. So we have everything from the demon of cancer to the demons of obesity, tobacco, unbelief, alcohol, sickness, and the like. Exorcise the demon and the believer will experience freedom from bondage.

Volumes in evangelical bookstores contain special prayers that serve as little more than religious incantations to bind these troubling demons and provide freedom. And if you need assistance along the way, don't forget: the angels are there to help.

One author described an angel that had one hundred nineteen clients, each of whom lived in a different galaxy. "The stubborn humans tend to ignore their angel guardians," he complains, "but this is not true for people on other planets. In fact, the dolphins and whales on earth stay in close contact with their angel friends."

A New Style of Religion?

Here is a telling statement of one author:

Those who focus on the spirit world naturally begin to associate every event with a spirit. From this arises the desire to know how to invoke the proper spirit for every need and also to learn the ritual that will thwart hurtful spirits. This is not just a phenomenon of the ancient world, but is the dark underside of centering one's life on the spirit world. I believe that this kind of religion is emerging from the present fascination with angels.

What does "touched by an angel" theology produce? It fosters a religion about *spirituality* rather than Jesus Christ. It is one that supposedly reveres God but never mentions the name of His Son.

Time Magazine reports:

For those who choke too easily on God and His rules, angels are the handy compromise. All fluff and meringue; kind; nonjudgmental. Like aspirin, they are available to everyone.

Another writer has said, "The search is on for spirituality, but *without* God."

So, angels provide all the wisdom, assistance, and religious connection you will ever need.

The Spiritual Profit from Studying Angels

When we begin to study what the Scriptures say about **angels, demons, and other flying creatures** in the spirit world, we find there are a number of benefits that come from a proper biblical understanding:

- **Increases of our appreciation of a sovereign God** – We will discover that angels do His bidding and demons are puppets on His string.

- **Comforts the believer** – Comfort for the Christian is not found in the availability of an angel but in the power of the Spirit of God Who indwells the believer.

- **Magnifies the patience of God with the world** – God could easily judge the world all at once. Yet, He waits, allowing evil men and demons alike to spite Him, hate Him, and seek to undermine Him and those who belong to Him.

- **Reminds the believer of spiritual warfare** – What is true spiritual warfare, and how is the Church distorting what is taught about it in the Scriptures? What are the dangers of taking fictional accounts like author Frank Peretti's and treating them like theology? I have read his works and they are very interesting fiction. There is a problem, however: a large portion of the Church has bought into them as if they were subjects of theology. As a result, there are prayers for the missions of angels, as well as prayers against territorial spirits.

- **Reveals an example of genuine worship** – Imagine being created to do nothing more than hover about the throne of God, singing at all times, "Holy, holy, holy." What submission to and utter reverence for our magnificent God! So often we go to God to get more *from* Him rather than to get more *of* Him. We are way more interested in what is *in* His hand than in His hand itself.

Challenges to Our Thoughts on Angels

As we begin our study, be prepared to have your thinking challenged (if it hasn't been already) concerning **angels, demons, and other flying creatures**.

Angels Probably Are Not Who You Think They Are

The biblical accounts of angels seem terrifying, especially to people to whom they were sent. In fact, their first words are usually something like, "Do not be afraid . . ." or "Fear not . . ."!

Furthermore, angels always seemed to be in a hurry. Several times their conversation began with words such as "Hurry and get up."

> **[A]n angel of the Lord spoke to Philip saying, "Get up and go . . . "** (Acts 8:26).

> **[A]n angel of the Lord suddenly appeared** [to Peter] **. . . saying, "Get up quickly"** (Acts 12:7).

C. S. Lewis laments how insipid our concept of angels has become over the years. He writes:

> *Fra Angelico's angels carry in their face and gesture the peace and authority of heaven. Later came the chubby and infantile nudes of Raphael; finally the soft, slim, girlish, and consolatory angels of nineteenth-century art. . . . In Scripture the visitation of an angel is always alarming; it has to begin by saying, "Fear not." The* [current] *angel looks as if it were going to say, "There, there."*

Yet, recorded in Revelation 19 and 22 twice, John the Apostle was touring heaven, encountered an angel, and immediately fell flat on his face. The angel told him to get up and stand on his feet.

One Old Testament account has one angel responsible for eliminating nearly 185,000 enemy soldiers, single-handedly (*2 Kings 19:35*).

In the New Testament, you may remember when the Roman soldiers came to arrest Christ in the Garden of Gethsemane, Peter pulled out his sword and cut off the ear of the high priest's servant. After Jesus healed the servant, He said,

"[D]o you think that I cannot appeal to My Father, and He will at once put at My disposal more than twelve legions of angels?" (Matthew 26:53).

There were six thousand Roman soldiers in a legion. Therefore, the Lord was referring to having at His disposal—at the snap of His finger—72,000 angels! If each of those angels could do what one angel in the Old Testament did, they could eliminate over thirteen billion people in an instant.

I hear many Christians wondering if Christianity is going to make it—we're so outnumbered by the forces of evil in our culture. Is anyone remembering the angels?!

Angels Probably Cannot Be Counted

The sheer number of angels speaks of God's immensity and glory. When John saw the throne of God with angels around it singing praise to the Lamb, he wrote:

[T]he number of them was ten thousand times ten thousand, and thousands of thousands (Revelation 5:11*b* KJV).

One author put it this way:

To put that into perspective, the average football stadium in America holds about fifty thousand people. It would take two thousand stadiums of that size to hold the angels John saw. For in his tour of heaven, he saw more than one hundred million angels.

Angels Are Intensely Curious about the Gospel

[I]n these things which now have been announced to you through those who preached the gospel to you by the Holy Spirit sent from heaven—things into which angels long to look (1 Peter 1:12).

The Greek words in this verse could be rendered, "The angels *stretch out their necks*; they bend downward to look into these things." Angels are fascinated with biblical truth!

Angels Are Incredibly Excited about Redemption

Jesus Christ said,

"[I] *tell you, there is joy in the presence of the angels of God over one sinner who repents"* (Luke 15:10).

There is an unbelievably joyful celebration among the angels over a single person who experiences redemption.

Why? Perhaps because they understand, by *sight*, the glory of God and the implications of eternity. They know that the sinner has been redeemed from the banishment from God's glory and the eternity of worship in heaven.

Angels Will Never Have a Personal Testimony of Redemption

Christ did not die for the angels. Angels do not trust Christ as Savior—they will not reign as joint heirs with Christ. We'll discuss this later in this study.

Angels Can Never Supplant Our Dependence on God

Has the Lord used angels as ministering agents in the lives of believers? Yes. But we are never told in Scripture to pray, "Lord, send an angel."

I believe that sometimes our Lord does use His angel servants to do His bidding on behalf of His sons and daughters.

John G. Paton, his wife, and his young child were missionaries to the New Hebrides Islands of the South Pacific a century ago. This account was given by tribesmen who later became Christians:

The Patons were encamped on the beach of an island that was populated by cannibals who had already killed visitors to their island. They prayed, went to sleep, and were not attacked by cannibals that night. Sometime later, after many of the natives came to faith in Christ, the Patons found that on that first night, the cannibals had indeed come to the beach to kill and eat them. But when they advanced upon the tiny camp, there suddenly appeared a great number of large warriors, each holding a drawn sword, surrounding the tent of the missionaries.

There is also the story of a group of missionaries who did die, and this amazing testimony came to light in the last few years:

Jim Elliott, Nate Saint, and three other men were missionaries who attempted to reach the Auca Indians of Ecuador with the Gospel. They had decided not to use their weapons, even if it meant they would die at the Indians' hands and, indeed, they were speared to death along a riverbank.

Many years later, as the Aucas came to faith in Christ, some of the older ones who had taken part in the killings told the account to Steve Saint, the son of Nate. They said that after all the men were speared to death, the Indians began to hear music. They looked above the tree line and saw a multitude of cowodi *(their word for missionary). They didn't recognize the music then, but later, when missionaries played recordings of Gospel choirs singing hymns of the faith, they knew those songs. Without a doubt, there at that riverbank, angels had come, singing and welcoming the martyrs to their eternal home.*

ANGELMANIA

Digging Deeper:

[T]hey were not serving themselves, but you, in these things which now have been announced to you through those who preached the gospel to you by the Holy Spirit sent from heaven—things into which angels long to look (1 Peter 1:12).

According to the following texts, what are some of the privileges we as Christians have that angels will never experience?

1 Peter 1:12

_____

_____

Galatians 4:4-6

_____

_____

Romans 8:16-17

_____

_____

What does Genesis 1:26-28 tell us about the advantages all human beings enjoy that the angelic world does not benefit from?

_____

_____

_____

_____

All Scripture is inspired by God and profitable for teaching, for reproof, for correction, for training in righteousness; so that the man of God may be adequate, equipped for every good work (2 Timothy 3:16).

There are many people who believe that angels provide a new source of additional wisdom. This view, however, denies the sufficiency of God's Word for our lives and contradicts one of the Bible's key doctrines known as the sufficiency of Scripture.

Read 2 Timothy 3:16 and then explain how this view of "additional" angelic wisdom conflicts with the doctrine of the sufficiency of God.

_____

_____

_____

_____

_____

What is the clear warning Paul issues in Galatians 1:8-10 about "new wisdom" from even an angelic source?

_____

_____

_____

Time Magazine reports, "For those who choke too easily on God and His rules, angels are the handy compromise: all fluff and meringue; kind, non-judgmental; like aspirin, they are available to everyone."

The world flocks to religions like this because they are not only warm and cozy, but they ignore the issue of sin.

What are some of the consequences that would result if we bought into the world system about God and His rules and we really served an "aspirin-like god," with no absolute laws or rules governing conduct.

_____

_____

_____

"In the same way, I tell you, there is joy in the presence of the angels of God over one sinner who repents" (Luke 15:10).

Isn't it fascinating that even though angels will never have the opportunity to experience redemption for themselves, they still humbly rejoice at the sight of our redemption? Why do you think they celebrate?

_____

_____

_____

In all of Scripture, we are never commanded or encouraged to pray, "Lord, send an angel." Even David, who went through a time of despair, never cried out for God to send an angel to comfort him. He simply reflected upon the character of God and continually praised Him for it.

Read David's prayer in Psalm 31:1-14, and then explain in your own words why the maturing believer doesn't pray for angels in times of trouble.

_____

_____

_____

_____

Take It to Heart:

Blessed be the God and Father of our Lord Jesus Christ, the Father of mercies and the God of all comfort; who comforts us in all our affliction so that we may be able to comfort those who are in affliction with the comfort with which we ourselves are comforted by God (2 Corinthians 1:3-4).

Where are the two sources of true comfort for the believer?

1._____

2._____

Write a prayer that follows this biblical example of David, which you can use in times of great trouble and affliction:

_____

_____

_____

_____

_____

_____

_____

_____

LEGENDS, FABLES, AND BIBLICAL ORIGINS

Without a doubt, interest in angels, demons, and other spirits or flying creatures is not new or unique to our generation. For instance, by the fourth century, praying to angels had so infiltrated and enamored the Church that a special church council was convened. This council, among other things, passed a resolution that forbade praying to angels.

The truth is, human nature wants something it can feel close to and even see. Of course we know that God cannot be seen by mortal eyes and often does not seem to be readily available or close by, so . . . angels are the next best thing.

Fascinating Legends, Fables, and Myths

The Legend of Tobias

The Apocryphal book of Tobit introduces an angel named Raphael, who calls himself "one of the seven holy angels who present the prayers of the saints and enter into the presence of the glory of the Holy One" (*Tobit 12:15 Apocrypha*).

The book of Tobit, by the way, was written by an unknown Jewish author two hundred years before the birth of Christ. It is so old—it even predates the incarnation of Christ! It has to be good, right?

Let's pause right here. "Old" is not necessarily right. Take a look at these examples of antiquity:

The Japanese have been involved in ancestral worship for a few thousand years and the Chinese have governed their lives around veneration for presumed patterns of negative and positive harmony flowing through nature and the body (yin and yang). The fact that these practices have been done for thousands of years does not mean they are anything other than pagan superstitions that were founded on the belief that divinity flows through everything and deceased relatives can open heaven.

Indians predated Europeans in North America. That does not mean that the Zodiac is the key to the heavens, Mother Earth should be worshiped, and animals are animated spirits. Granted, those concepts are ancient, but that does not mean they are purer or closer to the truth.

Ancient is not synonymous with wise. It just may be **old lies**.

Satan predates all offenses against monotheism, which is the worship of the one and only true and living God. Satan is really old and, in fact, he is the original liar.

Today, we have nothing but the **repackaging** of **old lies** in different forms, methods, and beliefs.

The legend from the book of Tobit is a good example:

Tobit was a Jew of exceptional piety, who lived among the exiles in Nineveh. Among his other labors of charity, Tobit took it upon himself to bury the body of any slain Jew he happened to come upon. One night his son Tobias told him that a fellow Jew had been strangled and left in the open marketplace. Tobit immediately went to take care of the situation. That night, because touching the corpse had made him unclean, he slept outside. At this point, Tobit fell victim to a tragic turn of events: bird droppings fell into his eyes and he went blind. (Isn't this a great legend?)

Meanwhile, in Ecbatana a young Jewish woman named Sarah had troubles of her own. Seven times she had married, and every time, the jealous demon Asmodeus had come and killed her new husband on their honeymoon night, just before they could consummate their marriage. Her reputation was in ruins. (I cannot imagine why!) Sarah didn't know what to do. In desperation she prayed for deliverance, and the angel Raphael stepped in.

It just so happened that Tobit—the blind guy—had business in Ecbatana, and his handsome young son Tobias was sent there to collect the money. The angel Raphael, disguised as a human, volunteered to escort Tobias. On the way to Ecbatana, they camped by the Tigris River and a fish jumped up from the river and tried to swallow Tobias. Raphael told Tobias to catch this man-eating fish, which he somehow accomplished. Raphael then instructed him to cut out the heart, liver, and gall, and keep them.

In Ecbatana, Raphael introduced Tobias to Sarah and told him she was just the girl for him. Tobias, however, had heard that she had been a somewhat "fatal attraction" for seven other men and politely refused. But Raphael persuaded him that she really was a wonderful girl and that Tobias could deal with the jealous demon quite easily. All he needed to do was take some hot ashes of incense into the bridal chamber and lay them on the heart and liver of the fish and the demon would flee. The marriage was arranged and, of course, Asmodeus came down to do away with Tobias.

When Asmodeus arrived, he smelled the burning fish heart and liver, which was fairly pungent by this time. He fled to Egypt where an angel bound him. This delighted Sarah's father, who had already dug grave number eight. Tobias picked up the money he had come for, returned to Nineveh and, using the fish gall on his father's eyes, healed Tobit's blindness. Thus Raphael earned the reputation as one of the greatest angels.

Well, dads, you now have a new bedtime story that will put your kids right to sleep. Of course, the lights will have to stay on all night throughout the entire house.

The Testament of Solomon

By the third century AD, the "Testament of Solomon" combined mysticism, Judaism, and Christianity to create a popular legend about the wisest man who ever lived—Solomon. This one will most definitely not be a good bedtime story:

The demon Ornias was sucking on the thumb of a little boy who was the son of the foreman of Solomon's temple construction project. As the boy began to languish and lose weight, Solomon prayed for help and Michael the Archangel came. Michael gave Solomon a ring that would allow him to bind all demons.

With the power of this ring, Solomon trapped and then interrogated the demon Ornias. He discovered that Ornias dwelt in Aquarius and could transform himself into a man, a winged creature, or a lion. During the interrogation, Solomon learned the names, astrological signs, and powers of the demons, as well as the names of the angels who could defeat them:

- **Onoskelis** *strangled men. Solomon captured her and made her forever sit at a weaver's shuttle and make things.*
- **Oropel** *gave people sore throats, but fled when the angel Raphael was invoked.*
- **Soubelti** *caused shivering and numbness, but retreated at the name of Rizoel.*
- **Anatreth** *gave people gas. (I am not making this up!) He would desist and leave people alone when they repeated, "Arara, Arare, Arara, Arare."*[1]

You could try that chant the next time you get indigestion. If it works, I do not want to know about it!

The legend ends with Solomon falling in love with Abishag the idolater. He sacrifices locust blood in order to win her love. God gets upset and Solomon loses control over all the demons and they are loosed again in the world.

The Legend of Metraton

In the days of the Apostle Paul, mixtures of paganism and Judaism had concocted all sorts of fanciful stories.

One example is the legend of Metraton, the ascended spirit of Enoch who had since become an angel and was responsible for directing millions of angels.

When the Dead Sea scrolls were discovered, several scrolls supposedly detailed deeper teaching. There was secret knowledge that involved sacred days in the calendar and, of course, details about the angels and spirit power.

Some of these early writers believed the ultimate discovery was to find a way to enable their souls to pierce the heavenly barrier and escape earth. Angels were an important part in helping spirits ascend. They viewed Jesus Christ as simply an ascended master who had arrived. It is interesting that two thousand years later, the New Age movement views Jesus Christ exactly the same way.

I repeat: this is **ancient stuff**—thousands of years old—but in reality, it is just **old lies**.

Paul saw all of these as myths and empty philosophies. No spirit master or angel wisdom helps the soul ascend to the next level of consciousness.

I believe that not only is the modern world filled with superstition and legends which are treated as doctrine, but the Church has equally fallen into a form of **dualism**: everything is a battle between good and evil spirits, with humans, unfortunately, caught in the middle. Humans are helpless and somewhat hopeless, unless the angels are stronger and more numerous than the demons. Demons are attached to everything bad and angels, to everything good. This sort of dualism has swept into the Church.

If you watch a televangelist, he may bind some invisible demon with an incantational prayer or heal someone by casting out the demon of cancer or high blood pressure.

I watched one program where the pastor gathered all the MasterCard and Visa balance sheets from people all around the country. He piled them in the church auditorium and proceeded to bind the demon of debt and set those people free.

What does that mean?! Do they not have to pay next month? No, of course not! This is as superstitious as the third-century belief that a demon causes indigestion.

Paul exhorted the believers:

> *Therefore as you have received Christ Jesus the Lord, so walk in Him, having been firmly rooted and now being built up in Him and established in your faith, just as you were instructed, and overflowing with gratitude. See to it that no one takes you captive through philosophy and empty deception, according to the tradition of men, according to the elementary principles of the world, rather than according to Christ. For in Him all the fullness of Deity dwells in bodily form, and in Him you have been made complete* (Colossians 2:6-10*a*).

In other words, you don't need secret knowledge to be made free in Christ. You don't need the help of angels against demons to make it through life or to be released from the demon of poverty. [A]*nd in Him you have been made complete* (Colossians 2:10*a*).

The word Paul uses for "complete" refers to the completeness of the believer whose **needs are fully met** through the exalted Lord.

In the Christian life, we don't need secret keys to get more of Christ (we have **all** of Christ already); the problem is that **He doesn't have all of us** due to our stubbornness and selfishness.

If we have a problem with MasterCard, it's because of materialism, not a demon. It's not the devil's fault—it's ours! But just like Eve of old: all the blame going to the devil (demons) has a wonderful way of letting us off the hook.

Forging Biblical Sense from Nonsense

To find biblical sense, let's begin by going back to the time of creation.

Angels Had a Moment of Origin

Praise Him, all His angels; praise Him, all His hosts!
Praise Him, sun and moon; praise Him, all stars of light!
Let them praise the name of the LORD, for He commanded
and they were created (Psalm 148:2-3, 5).

In the beginning was the Word, and the Word was with God,
and the Word was God. He was in the beginning with God.
All things came into being through Him, and apart from Him
nothing came into being that has come into being (John 1:1-3).

For by Him all things were created, both in the heavens and
on earth, visible and invisible, whether thrones or dominions
or rulers or authorities—all things have been created through
Him and for Him. He is before all things, and in Him all
things hold together (Colossians 1:16-17).

These passages inform us that all the angels were created by Jesus Christ—the Divine Agent in creation.

Angels Were Created before Anything Else
and Witnessed the Wonder of Creation

Where were you when I laid the foundation of the earth?
Tell Me, if you have understanding, who set its measurements?
Since you know. Or who stretched the line on it? On what were
its bases sunk? Or who laid its cornerstone, when the morning

stars sang together and all the sons of God shouted for joy (Job 38:4-7)***?***

This is a reference to the angels shouting for joy and singing as a response to the creative acts of God.

I was asked the question as to whether or not angels have souls. We are not specifically told this, but the angels exhibit the activities that we normally attribute to the soul: mind, emotions, and will.

Angels Were Created with Intelligence

We are told that angels are fascinated with the doctrine of our salvation and desire to learn about redemption—***things into which angels long to look*** (1 Peter 1:12).

This lets us know that though angels may be smart, they are not omniscient; they cannot read our mind; they do not know the future unless God has revealed it to them.

However, they are incredibly brilliant, and they've had several thousand years to grow even smarter!

God told Satan,

Your heart was lifted up because of your beauty; you corrupted your wisdom by reason of your splendor (Ezekiel 28:17*a*).

Angels Were Created with Emotions

Angels:

* shouted for joy at God's creative acts (*Job 38:7*);
* worship God with awe and humility (*Isaiah 6:3*);
* recognize the deity of Christ and worship the Lamb, ascribing to Him blessing and honor and glory and power (*Revelation 5:13*);
* rejoice when a sinner comes to faith in Christ (*Luke 15:10*).

From these verses, we can conclude that angels are not robotic beings who are without thought or feeling.

Angels Were Created with a Will

Angels have what theologians call self-determination: they can choose from various courses of action and seek to carry out one. They were created to know, understand, and obey the will of God intelligently and faithfully.

When we look at the record of Lucifer's fall (we will, in more detail later in this study), five times Lucifer said, "I will . . ."

"But you said in your heart, 'I will ascend to heaven; I will raise my throne above the stars of God, and I will sit on the mount of assembly in the recesses of the north. I will ascend above the heights of the clouds; I will make myself like the Most High'" (Isaiah 14:13-14).

"I will . . . I will . . . I will . . . I will . . . I will . . . " On that basis, he chose to defect and millions of angels went with him.

Angels Made the Choice to Defect and Sealed Their Destiny

The choice of angels to defect confirmed their judgment and, according to Matthew 25:41, they are already guaranteed an eternal future in hell.

Luke 20:36 states that once created, the angels—both holy and fallen—will never cease to exist; they are immortal.

Can a demon or an angel be saved? No. Angels do not repent and are not redeemed. Hebrews 2:14-18 makes it clear that redemption is for humanity, not angelic beings.

The angels who chose to follow God (more than two-thirds of them) were likewise **confirmed in holiness**, not **redeemed**.

When did this choice take place in the world of angelic beings? When did the great rebellion occur? We are not told exactly when, but putting the clues together, we arrive at these conclusions:

1. Angels were created before the first chapter of Genesis (*Job 38:4-7*);
2. Satan was present in the Garden of Eden to tempt Eve (*Genesis 3*).

Thus, angels either chose to rebel or follow God during the time between the six days of Creation and Genesis 3, or at some point during Genesis 2. So, if you can determine how much time elapses in Genesis— or to put it another way, how long Adam and Eve lived in the Garden of Eden—you will have the answer.

The "Legend of Enoch" has the answer: Adam and Eve were only able to hold on to the Garden of Eden for five hours. This is fanciful, of course. Genesis 2 records that Adam had enough time to name all the animal species, realize he was missing his other half, have major surgery to remove a rib, have a wedding ceremony with the woman he named Eve, and still have time left over to get talked into eating some fruit he never should have eaten. To accomplish all that would certainly take more than five hours! We can say this with certainty: angels made their choice prior to the Fall of Man.

How Do Angels Serve?

Angels Serve with Passion

If we can learn anything from angels, it is that they serve God with great passion. The fallen angels **hate** God with passion; the holy angels **love** Him and serve Him with great passion.

If angels had a mission statement, it would be "Passionately Serving God."

Angels Serve with Privileges

Imagine what the angels see! Imagine what they know! They are so close to the throne and the things of God.

Angels Serve with Purpose

1. **Angels exalt the character of God.**

   Then I looked, and I heard the voice of many angels around the throne and the living creatures and the elders; and the number of them was myriads of myriads, and thousands of thousands, saying with a loud voice, "Worthy is the Lamb that was slain to receive power and riches and wisdom and might and honor and glory and blessing." And every created thing which is in heaven and on the earth and under the earth and on the sea, and all things in them, I heard saying, "To Him who sits on the throne, and to the Lamb, be blessing and honor and glory and dominion forever and ever." And the four living creatures kept saying, "Amen" (Revelation 5:11-14*a*).

2. **Angels execute the will of God.**
   We will look at this in later chapters.

3. **Angels enforce the judgment of God.**

They do this by:

- chastising believers (*2 Samuel 24*);
- punishing unbelievers (*Genesis 19* – God used angels in the condemnation of Sodom and Gomorrah);
- destroying earth's resources (*Revelation* – the incredible power of angels is revealed as they destroy much of planet Earth during the Great Tribulation);
- casting unbelieving humanity, after the final judgment, into the lake of fire (*Matthew 13:49-50; Revelation 20:15*).

The end of the kingdom is foretold:

"So it will be at the end of the age; the angels shall come forth and take out the wicked from among the righteous, and will throw them into the furnace of fire; in that place there will be weeping and gnashing of teeth" (Matthew 13:49-50).

And if anyone's name was not found written in the book of life, he was thrown into the lake of fire (Revelation 20:15).

What a horrifying moment it will be as the history of time ends and eternity begins. The **great white throne** of God will thunder the word, "Guilty!" and all the unredeemed will kneel and every tongue will cry out, "You are Lord! We know and believe now that You are Lord!"

Then the angels will swoop down upon billions of unredeemed from all time, pick them up, and throw them into hell.

Three Points to Remember

These three points should help you sift the sense from the nonsense:

1. **To depend on the activity of angels is to dilute the power of God.**

The Apostle Paul said, *I can do all things through Him [Christ] who strengthens me* (Philippians 4:13).

He wrote his personal testimony to the Corinthian believers:

And He has said to me, "My grace is sufficient for you, for power is perfected in weakness." Most gladly, therefore, I will rather boast about my weaknesses, so that the power of Christ may dwell in me (2 Corinthians 12:9).

2. **To concentrate on the role of angels will diminish our relationship with Christ.**

   [F]*ixing our eyes on Jesus, the author and perfecter of faith . . .* (Hebrews 12:2*a*).

   The word "fixing" is *aphorao* in the Greek, and means **to concentrate on Jesus Christ**. Jesus said, *"And I, if I am lifted up from the earth, will draw all men to Myself"* (John 12:32). Our focus should be on Christ and not the spirit beings He created.

3. **The believer's responsibility is not to determine which stories are true, but to rightly divide the *Word of truth*.**

   Dorothy Maclean and her colleagues apparently had spectacular success with their gardens in Scotland. They wrote a book about their alleged secret: she had learned to communicate with the angels of her plants! "I would get centered on my higher self through meditation and then address a question to the angel of a particular species of plant." She found that "the being behind the garden pea held the design of all pea plants in a sort of inner energy stream of divinity."

I know this cannot be true! There is no such thing as an angel of garden peas or, at least *if* an angel is responsible for peas, it would be a fallen angel! That one is easy.

We are not told to be expert students of legends, but we are told:

> **Study to show yourself approved unto God, a workman that need not to be ashamed, rightly dividing the word of truth** (2 Timothy 2:15 KJV).

The next verse is very interesting, in light of our study:

> **But avoid worldly and empty chatter, for it will lead to further ungodliness, and their talk will spread like gangrene** (2 Timothy 2:16-17a).

We are told to avoid empty chatter, which literally means "empty sounds"—chatter that is **interesting** but **empty**. Consider the chatter of

Tobias and Sarah, the Testament of Solomon, the Books of Enoch—interesting but empty.

Stay close to the Bible—this Book of divine origin. Study it, and in so doing, not only will you discover the truth, but you will also be protected against all sorts of legends and myths.

God has not told us everything about the unseen world of **angels, demons, and other flying creatures**, but He has told us **everything we need to know**!

LEGENDS, FABLES, AND BIBLICAL ORIGINS

Digging Deeper:

You have learned in this chapter about **dualism**—the belief that humans are hopelessly stuck in the middle of a great battle between demons and angels. Dualists credit all the negative experiences of life to demons and all the positive experiences to angels.

According to James 1:2-3, trials and negative experiences can actually be used by God to develop character. In addition, Job 1 tells us that trials cannot come to a believer without God's permission.

Therefore, no matter what experiences you may have, God has your **development** in mind, while Satan has your **destruction** in mind.

What trials are you currently experiencing?

_____

_____

_____

_____

Which result seems to be occurring in your life: destruction or development?

_____

A principle to keep in mind: **The work of God in your heart will always lead to hope; the whispers of Satan in your heart will always lead to despair.**

Therefore as you have received Christ Jesus the Lord, so walk in Him, having been firmly rooted and now being built up in Him and established in your faith, just as you were instructed, and overflowing with gratitude.

See to it that no one takes you captive through philosophy and empty deception, according to the tradition of men, according to the elementary principles of the world, rather than according to Christ. For in

***Him all the fullness of Deity dwells in bodily form, and in Him you
have been made complete, and He is the head over all rule and authority*** (Colossians 2:6-10).

Based on what you've just read, describe what this text would say about
dualism . . . and other similar religions.

_____

_____

_____

_____

Based on these few verses, decide for yourself if you really are just a helpless, hopeless person whose entire existence rests upon whether or not the
angelic forces outnumber the demonic forces. Find key words and phrases
in Colossians 2:6-10 that combat this false belief of dualism.

List key words that communicate who you really are.

_____

_____

_____

_____

_____

**[F]*or by Him all things were created, both in the heavens and on
earth, visible and invisible, whether thrones or dominions or rulers or
authorities—all things have been created through Him and for Him.
He is before all things, and in Him all things hold together*** (Colossians
1:16-17).

Where do angels come from?

_____

_____

When did they come into being? (note the presence of the angels at creation [*Job 38:4-7*])

_____

_____

***"So it will be at the end of the age; the angels will come forth and take
out the wicked from among the righteous, and will throw them into***

***the furnace of fire; in that place there will be weeping and gnashing of
teeth"*** (Matthew 13:49-50).

In the previous chapter you read a quote from *Time Magazine* which
said that angels are a great replacement for God because they are never
judgmental; they are always kind and compassionate, and they overlook
sin rather than dealing with it. How does the **truth** of this text contradict
the world's misconception of angels?

_____

_____

_____

_____

According to Revelation 20:11-15, when will the angels cast the unbelieving into the lake of fire?

_____

_____

_____

Take It to Heart:

Paul warns the believer to avoid the popular trends and speculations of
our world . . . especially the fanciful trends regarding the spiritual world
of angels and demons.

***But avoid worldly and empty chatter, for it will lead to further ungod-
liness, and their talk will spread like gangrene . . .*** (2 Timothy 2:16-
17*a*).

We are commanded as Christians to avoid empty chatter or empty
sounds—that is, chatter which is interesting but empty. What are some
examples from our current culture that would fall under the category
of interesting but empty chatter about the spirit world (whether from a
popular author, best-seller, or the media)?

_____

_____

_____

_____

Memorize Philippians 4:13:
"I can do all things through Christ who strengthens me."

And remember, it is God's power **alone** that can give you the strength to live each day. Don't look to yourself for your source of spiritual strength and power . . . and definitely never look to the angels!

GUARDIANS AND GALLANT WARRIORS

Close Encounters?

In *Henry IV*, Shakespeare has two people conversing. The first says, "I can call spirits from the vast deep." The other responds, "Why, so can I, or so can any man, but will they come when you call for them?"

From Shakespeare to Hollywood, the public has always been, and always will be, fascinated with the prospect of an encounter with an angel or any being from the spirit world.

John Randolph Price writes what he considers to be a surefire four-step approach to accessing angels:

1. Scan your consciousness for anything negative or shameful from the past and cast it all on the love of God within yourself;

2. Look for negative traits, such as jealousy, resentment, and anger outside of yourself;

3. Make a surrender of mind, emotions, and body to the spirit within;

4. Meditate.

Having done all the above, you can be sure that an angel encounter is near. He continues, "At a certain point you will see a light up ahead, and you will know that you are approaching the angel."

In *Ask Your Angels*, the reader is given a lot of methods and exercises for making angel contact, and they all revolve around the acrostic GRACE:

- G – Grounding
- R – Releasing
- A – Aligning
- C – Conversing
- E – Enjoying

Ask Your Angels gives a five-step program to getting what you want in life and tells the way in which the spirit world can deliver it:

1. Make a deliberate choice about what you want;

2. Commit to getting it;

3. Visualize the goal;
4. Give thanks to the "Source of All";
5. Release the goal to the Universe so it can then take over and deliver what you've ordered.

This convoluted spirit "wishing" has already become a fad. It has been refined and adopted in the Church under the guise of **prosperity theology**. It parades across the church platforms of America. The only difference is those churches insert God's name in steps four and five!

In other words, "Name it; claim it; God will deliver it!"

This prosperity movement asserts that one way God delivers is through angels.

It may sound spiritual and biblical terminology might be used, but it is nothing more than **religious materialism**. In reality, it is a doctrine of demons, and it merely enslaves a person to the idols of materialism in the name of God. It horribly reduces God to a cosmic genie who grants your wish any time you rub the magic lamp.

I'm Dreaming of . . .

One of the things these authors emphasize is that you should accept your dreams as being messages from the angels.

It won't be long before we will have experts telling Christians how to interpret their dreams. They will be calling their seminars and conferences names such as "How to Dream like Daniel," "The Wisdom of Joseph for Today," and "Turning Dreams into Deliverance." Mark my words, this is the next fad "Coming Soon to a Church Near You!"

A lady came to me some time ago and said, "Stephen, I had a dream the other night and you were in it."

I asked, "Really?"

She replied, "Yes, I dreamed that you were dialing heaven on a telephone; you were going to call God and you knew the number!" She continued, "You dialed 3-6-2 but I couldn't make out the other numbers."

I told her to go back and dream some more—I want the rest of that phone number!

Let no one keep defrauding you of your prize by delighting in self-abasement and the worship of the angels, taking his stand on visions he has seen, inflated without cause by his fleshly mind (Colossians 2:18).

In other words, do not base your theology on angels and visions.

Special Consignment: On the Wings of Angels

Let's look at several things the Bible clearly teaches about the ministry of angels.

Angels Obey the Commands of God

The word "angel" comes from the Greek word *angelos*, and it simply means messenger. Often throughout Scripture, they are obeying the commands of God by delivering messages.

In the Old Testament angels constantly arrived with messages for the servants of God. One of the most interesting accounts is in Numbers 22. An angel was sent to stop Balaam, the prophet who was willing to curse Israel for the right price. The angel blocked the way of the donkey carrying Balaam. When Balaam began to beat the donkey, it turned another way. The angel again stood in the way, causing the donkey to press against a stone wall, and in so doing, squash Balaam's foot. Balaam angrily continued to beat the donkey, and it tried to go another way. Finding the angel once again in front of it, the poor donkey finally just lay down. The angel then became visible to Balaam who, at that moment, became as spiritually discerning as his donkey!

Now many have wrongly concluded from this account that animals can see the spirit world. Some artists enjoy painting pictures of angels in which the dog by the bedside of a departing saint sees the angel, while the family grieves their loss.

Part of God's judgment on Balaam was first delivered by stopping his donkey. This implies that God can work through a donkey just as easily as He can work through His prophet! God can give insight into the spirit world to a dumb animal if He so chooses.

The point for Balaam was that he needed to stop acting like a stubborn donkey and start acting like an obedient prophet. And if he did, God would give him supernatural discernment as well.

In the New Testament, the activity of angels does not slow down. In fact, while angels are mentioned 108 times in the Old Testament, they are cited 165 times in the New Testament.

Angels were perhaps never more busy than around the time of the birth of Jesus Christ. An angel:

- appeared to Zacharias to tell him that his wife Elizabeth would have a son, and that they should name him John—he would become John the Baptist. Zacharias doubted the angelic messenger and the angel struck him mute (*Luke 1*);
- delivered the message to Mary that she, a virgin, would conceive by the Holy Spirit and bear a son. She believed the messenger and, unlike her relative Zacharias, was able to talk about it (*Luke 1*);
- anonymously appeared to Joseph in a dream and explained the details of Mary's pregnancy, which had obviously troubled this young fiancé (*Matthew 1*);
- appeared in heavenly glory to a group of shepherds who were stunned and afraid. Then the angel was suddenly joined by as many as tens of thousands who began to chant in unison that the Savior had just been born (*Luke 2*);
- came to Joseph and warned him to flee from Herod to Egypt with Mary and Jesus and later told Joseph that Herod was dead and he could return home (*Matthew 2*).

And of the angels He says, "Who makes His angels winds, and His ministers a flame of fire" (Hebrews 1:7).

David wrote:

The LORD has established His throne in the heavens, and His sovereignty rules over all. Bless the LORD, you His angels, mighty in strength, who perform His word, obeying the voice of His word! Bless the LORD, all you His hosts, you who serve Him, doing His will (Psalm 103:19-21).

Dear reader, you need to remember:

- angels are not summoned by the wishes of man; they are sent by the will of God;
- angels do not come down by the special prayers of man; they come down for the special purposes of God.

However, make no mistake—angels do more than run a delivery service for the King of heaven.

Angels Deliver the Judgments of God

The plagues of Egypt prior to the Israelite exodus from slavery are set forth in this passage:

When He performed His signs in Egypt, and His marvels in the field of Zoan, and turned their rivers to blood, and their streams, they could not drink. He sent among them swarms of flies, which devoured them, and frogs which destroyed them. He gave also their crops to the grasshopper, and the product of their labor to the locust. He destroyed their vines with hailstones, and their sycamore trees with frost. He gave over their cattle also to the hailstones, and their herds to bolts of lightning. He sent upon them His burning anger, fury, and indignation and trouble, a band of destroying angels (Psalm 78:43-49).

One of the most graphic descriptions of angelic power sent from God to judge a human being is found in the Acts of the Apostles:

On an appointed day Herod, having put on his royal apparel, took his seat on the rostrum and began delivering an address to them (Acts 12:21).

You need to understand that this is the same Herod who had recently put James to death in order to gain the support of the Jews. He knew the Jews would honor him for putting to death a leader of the divisive new sect that followed a criminal they had executed on a cross some months earlier.

Herod had so pleased the Jews that he also put Peter in prison, intending to do the same to him.

Now notice how the people responded to Herod's speech:

The people kept crying out, "The voice of a god and not of a man!" (Acts 12:22).

Obviously Herod reveled in this form of demigod worship. But God had other lessons to teach, as well as a plan to protect the Church from further executions of its leaders at that time:

And immediately an angel of the Lord struck him because he did not give God the glory, and he was eaten by worms and died. But the word of the Lord continued to grow and to be multiplied (Acts 12:23-24).

The king was probably killed by intestinal roundworms which can grow to a length of ten to fourteen inches. Clusters of roundworms can obstruct the intestine and cause severe pain and ultimate death.

Following Herod's death, the Church experienced further growth and the Word of God found receptive hearts everywhere.

You cannot help but see the contrast here. There is the growth and multiplication of **worms, which bring death,** and the counterpoint of the growth and multiplication of the **Word, which brings life.**

The angel's judgment of worms against Herod is a graphic picture of the torment of hell:

[T]*o be cast into hell,* [is to enter a place] ***where their worm does not die, and the fire is not quenched*** (Mark 9:47*b*-48).

The word for worms in Acts 12 is the same word used in Mark 9. We may ask, "How could God ever devise such a terrible place of punishment?"

That shouldn't be the question. We have already been told that hell is designed for the devil and his angels (*Matthew 25:41*).

The really mind-blowing question to me is, "How could you ever read about this place, be warned of its torment, be given a description of its anguish and, yet, still refuse to admit your sinfulness and accept the gift of eternal life through faith in Jesus Christ?"

At that moment King Herod became a description of humanity that worships itself and suffers hell. Josephus, the first-century Jewish historian, wrote about this event with some detail:

Herod Agrippa was "overcome by more intense pain, exhausted after five straight days by the pain in the abdomen; he departed this life in the fifty-fourth year of his life."[2]

Now, don't make the mistake of thinking that this was the independent idea of the angel, as if he were thinking, "Hey, I think I'll give Herod worms." No, this was God's idea—and the angel was given the power to deliver the judgment.

As frightening as this account may be, it is equally comforting to know that while angels can be a terror to the enemies of God, they can be protectors and servants of God's children as well.

Angels Assist the Lives of Believers

You may recall that just before Herod met his death by worms, he had placed Peter in prison to gain even more points in the popularity polls.

So Peter was kept in the prison, but prayer for him was being made fervently by the church to God. On the very night when Herod was about to bring him forward, Peter was sleeping between two soldiers, bound with two chains; and guards in front of the door were watching over the prison. And behold, an angel of the Lord suddenly appeared, and a light shone in the cell; and he struck Peter's side and woke him up, saying, "Get up quickly." And his chains fell off his hands (Acts 12:5-7).

That was not a very nice way to wake someone. The angel said, "Don't just stand there Peter, get dressed!"

And the angel said to him, "Gird yourself and put on your sandals." And he did so. And he said to him, "Wrap your cloak around you and follow me." And he went out and continued to follow, and he did not know that what was being done by the angel was real, but thought he was seeing a vision. When they had passed the first and second guard, they came to the iron gate that leads into the city, which opened for them by itself; and they went out and went along one street, and immediately the angel departed from him. When Peter came to himself, he said, "Now I know for sure that the Lord has sent forth His angel and rescued me (Acts 12:8-11a).

I just can't help but say, "No, Peter—really? What was your first clue?" I love that he said, "*Now* I know for sure."

He is not the only one in this story who is slow to catch on! While Peter has been sleeping in the prison, the believers are elsewhere, dozing through a prayer meeting. They look intense, but they are just mouthing the words. They are gathered and are praying, no doubt, for Peter's rescue.

And when he realized this, he went to the house of Mary, the mother of John who was also called Mark, where many were gathered together and were praying. When he knocked at the door of the gate, a servant-girl named Rhoda came to answer. And when she recognized Peter's voice, because of her joy she did not open the gate, but ran in and announced that Peter was standing in front of the gate. And they said to her, "You are out of your mind!" (Acts 12: 12-15a).

I can just hear them saying, "Listen, we're trying to pray for Peter and you're interrupting us with some wild story. Now, calm down. Let's see, where were we? Oh yeah, 'And Lord, help Peter!'"

But she kept insisting that it was so. They kept saying, "It is his angel." But Peter continued knocking; and when they had opened the door, they saw him and were amazed (Acts 12:15b-16).

This is encouraging. If you ever get caught up in the false teaching that God only answers prayers that you pray with unwavering faith, then read through this text a few times. If you ever think that God is not really listening to you because you have not mastered the art of praying without doubting, then take a close look at this prayer meeting.

They finally open the door to close Rhoda's mouth, poor girl, and there stands Peter! And they were amazed: "What do you know?! God answered *our* prayers!"

By the way, much speculation has been based on the fact that these believers said, *"It is his angel"* (Acts 12:15c).

Many would say that this is proof that every believer has an angel guarding him—otherwise known as their guardian angel.

There is a big difference between what the Bible reports at times and what the Bible teaches us to do. There is a difference between what the Bible **communicates** and what it **commands**.

The Bible, in this verse, is simply giving us the response of these people. It is not necessarily telling us that their response was the truth.

Then to what does this refer? If you go back to the beliefs of Judaism, around the first century especially, it was commonly held that a guardian angel was assigned to each believer. It was also thought that the guardian angel took on the appearance of their human charge and even went so far as to mimic the human's voice.

While the Bible never tells us this is true, it simply reports that these Jewish believers thought it was true.

But what about Psalm 91:11?

That verse tells us **He will give His angels charge concerning you, to guard you in all your ways** (Psalm 91:11).

This verse definitely teaches that angels are servants of God to guard the believer, but it doesn't say that we each have an angel. It tells us that **all believers have all the angels**. The entire host of heaven is devoted to seeing the will of God carried out on earth, and no demon, no event, no tragedy, no obstacle can keep God's will from being performed in and through our lives.

The reformer John Calvin said that if a believer cannot take assurance that all the angels are aiding the life of the believer in unseen ways, certainly he will take no comfort in believing that only one angel is so assigned.

There are two other verses that indicate the angelic collaboration with the Triune God in serving the believer:

> **But to which of the angels has He ever said, "Sit at My right hand, until I make your enemies a footstool for your feet"? Are they not all ministering spirits, sent out to render service for the sake of those who will inherit salvation** (Hebrews 1:13-14)?

We are not told how, where, or when. We are certainly never told to pray to them, to look for them, or to depend on them. God simply uses angels to perform His will on behalf of the believer, whenever He chooses.

Corrie ten Boom was raised in Amsterdam. Her family was sent to a concentration camp for hiding Jews in their home during the terror of Hitler. I have had the privilege of touring that home. I walked up the stairs to her bedroom, which housed a small linen closet that served as the door to a space where Jews hid when the German soldiers came to search the house.. Corrie's family was discovered, and they were sent to Ravensbrueck. This is one account of the time when Corrie and her sister Betsie arrived at the concentration camp:

> *It was very cold and the sisters had already spent two days and nights outside. They were waiting in line to get into the administration building. There the Nazis were taking all the possessions of the new arrivals, including their clothes, and giving them only a thin dress,*

an undershirt, and a pair of wooden shoes. When they got into the building, Corrie had an inspiration. She instructed Betsie to take off her woolen undergarments, roll them up, and put them in a corner. She whispered to Betsie, "The Lord is busy answering our prayers. We shall not have to make the sacrifice of all our clothes."

After they had been undressed, showered, and handed the shabby clothes, Corrie writes, "I hid the roll of underwear under my dress. It bulged out obviously through my thin dress, but I prayed, 'Lord, surround me with angels so the guards cannot see me.'" The guards checked everyone. Not a bulge escaped their eyes. The woman just in front of me had hidden a woolen vest under her dress; it was taken from her. They let me pass by; they obviously did not even see me. Betsie, right behind me, was searched. But outside awaited another danger. On each side of the door were women who looked everyone over a second time. They felt over the body of each one who passed. I knew they would not see me, for I was still surrounded. I was not even surprised when they passed right by me, but within me rose the jubilant cry, "O Lord, if Thou does so answer prayer, I can face even Ravensbrueck unafraid."

There is another verse that is so intriguing to me:

Let love of the brethren continue. Do not neglect to show hospitality to strangers, for by this some have entertained angels without knowing it (Hebrews 13:2).

What an interesting motive for demonstrating love. We might be ministering to an angel who has taken human form to receive from us the proof of our salvation: love for one another.

The operative phrase in this verse is "without knowing it." The verb and the tense indicate that the person never knew it happened—not during and not after. That seems to take care of a lot of interesting stories in which the person discovers it a second later.

This verse is saying we should demonstrate our love, and we may even entertain angels without ever knowing it—at least until we get to heaven, when our faithfulness is rewarded by God.

Angels Control the Kingdom of Satan

And there was war in heaven, Michael and his angels waging war with the dragon. And the dragon and his angels waged war, and they were not strong enough, and there was no longer a place found for them in heaven. And the great dragon was thrown down, the serpent of old who is called the devil and Satan, who deceives the whole world; he was thrown down to the earth, and his angels were thrown down with him (Revelation 12:7-9).

And I saw an angel coming down from heaven, having the key of the abyss and a great chain in his hand. And he laid hold of the dragon, the serpent of old, who is the devil and Satan, and bound him for a thousand years, and threw him into the abyss, and shut it and sealed it over him, so that he would not deceive the nations any longer, until the thousand years were completed; after these things he must be released for a short time (Revelation 20:1-3).

Do you have a guess on how many angels it will take to throw Satan into the abyss at the end of the Tribulation? How many angels had to get together to take on the dragon?

One. Only one angel, empowered by God, will be sufficient to toss the old dragon into the pit. Just one!

The theology of today, based on stories and fiction, seems to indicate that the angels might lose—that they're outnumbered and underdeveloped— and believers are in danger because there are not enough mighty angels around to help.

This is not so, according to the record of Scripture. When the history of the world comes to its end, just one anonymous angel will cast Satan into the abyss and, ultimately, into the lake of fire.

Special Citation: Angels Up Close

For further study on your own, the following are passages of Scripture where angels and other flying creatures are mentioned.

Cherubim

Ezekiel 1 describes the vision of the cherubim having the form of man with four different faces (human, lion, bull, and eagle) turned to the four compass directions. They can take off in any direction without ever having to turn their faces or their bodies, and their wings make the sound of a waterfall.

Seraphim

Isaiah 6 gives the account of these beings with three pairs of wings, who fly about the throne of God chanting, "Holy, Holy, Holy . . . "

Michael the Archangel

Of all the hundreds of millions of angels, both fallen and holy, we are given the names of only three of them: Lucifer (Satan), Michael the Archangel, and Gabriel.

Michael is mentioned in Daniel 10, Jude 9, and Revelation 12. He is commonly seen as a warrior and may very well be the general of God's army of warrior angels.

Gabriel

Gabriel is constantly showing up with messages. In Daniel 9, he had a message for Daniel, and for Zacharias and Mary in Luke 1.

Other Angel Moments

Other angel sightings that are biblically based are found when you study:

- the **rapture** of the church (*1 Thessalonians 4:16*);
- the **tribulation** on planet earth (*Revelation 16*);
- the **final battle** against hell (*Revelation 20*);
- the **final execution** of **God's judgment** (*Revelation 20:15*).

Three Final Thoughts on Holy Angels

1. Their **service** is largely unseen by the Christian.
2. Their **obedience** is absolutely exemplary for the believer.
3. Their **victory** has been totally guaranteed by God.

Guardians and Gallant Warriors

Digging Deeper:

Let no one keep defrauding you of your prize by delighting in self-abasement and the worship of the angels, taking his stand on visions he has seen, inflated without cause by his fleshly mind, and not holding fast to the head, from whom the entire body, being supplied and held together by joints and ligaments, grows with a growth which is from God (Colossians 2:18-19).

What are some of the ways that can lead to our deception and idolatry?

_____

_____

_____

_____

According to these verses, where should we place our focus and derive our beliefs? (Read also *Colossians 2:8-10*)

_____

_____

For He will give His angels charge concerning you, to guard you in all your ways (Psalm 91:11).

Does this verse imply that we each have a guardian angel watching over us at all times, or more than one? Compare this verse to Hebrews 1:13-14 and then explain your answer.

But to which of the angels has He ever said, "Sit at My right hand, until I make your enemies a footstool for your feet"? Are they not all ministering spirits, sent out to render service for the sake of those who will inherit salvation (Hebrews 1:13-14)?

_____

_____

_____

_____

What are some biblical examples that you can think of where God used angels to either carry out a message or to minister to one of His children?

Reference:

_____

Reference:

_____

Reference:

_____

Reference:

_____

Take It to Heart:

Let love of the brethren continue. Do not neglect to show hospitality to strangers, for by this some have entertained angels without knowing it (Hebrews 13:1-2).

Think of all of the events that have taken place in your life in the past week. Have you shown hospitality to any strangers? What about in the past month . . . or past year?

Briefly describe at least one occasion where you did something kind for a stranger and no one noticed or patted you on the back for it.

_____

_____

_____

_____

Who knows? Maybe you took the opportunity to help at least one person . . . he or she may have been a messenger from heaven!

Regardless of whether or not this stranger *was* an angel, you have actually served the Lord Himself! He said, *"Inasmuch as you did it to one of the least of these My brethren* (referring to the homeless guy on the street or the lady at the grocery store)*, you did it unto Me"* (Matthew 25:40).

Now that's motivation for showing hospitality to strangers! Wouldn't you rather entertain Christ at your house than an angel? How about it . . . who are you going to entertain this week?

THE FALLEN CHERUB

Going to the Dark Side

Forty years ago, C. S. Lewis, author of *Mere Christianity*, wrote these provocative words:

> *There are two equal and opposite errors into which our race can fall with regard to devils. One is to disbelieve in their existence. The other is to believe, and to feel an excessive and unhealthy interest in them. The demons are equally pleased by both errors, and welcome a materialist or magician with the same delight.*[3]

I, personally, believe he is right.

On one hand is the **materialist**, as Lewis called him. This is the person who either denies the reality of Satan and his power or simply lives with such spiritual lethargy and complacency that he never engages in the discipline of spiritual warfare. He does not invest his time, energy, prayer, and resources in advancing the Church of Jesus Christ.

This is the liberal who denies the reality of hell and demons and Satan. They like to talk of hell as a concept and Satan as a mythical power or evil force but not a literal person.

Vance Havner, a famous twentieth-century evangelist, once preached,

> *If the Devil comes to town in a body, you won't likely find him in a nightclub or a gambling dive. The world and the flesh will look after these places. You'll more likely find the devil in some pulpit, with an education, drawing a salary for denying his own (Satan's) existence.*[4]

One such minister was preaching that the word "in" does not necessarily mean "in." So when the Bible says that Jonah went down in the whale, the word "in" simply means "close to, round about, or nearby." After the service a man complimented him on the finest sermon he said he had ever heard. He went on to say how much it encouraged him and cleared up so many other mysteries he had encountered in the Bible: "For instance, the story about the three young Hebrew boys who were thrown *in* the fiery furnace but were not burned. Now I see that they were not really in the fire, just close to, round about, or nearby. And the story about Daniel getting thrown into the lion's den. Now I see that he was not really thrown *in* the lion's den, but close to it. But," he said, "the most encouraging thing is that even though I am a wicked man, I am gratified to know that I won't actually be *in* hell, just close to, round about, or nearby."

It is easy to understand why the materialist view which denies the personality of Satan and the reality of hell would be so popular!

On the other hand is the **magician**, as Lewis called him, or the **mystic** who believes in the demonic world and sees a demon behind every bush and Satan behind every event. He becomes so fascinated with the demon world that his world revolves around conflict with them.

It is not uncommon to hear mystical leaders speak of breaking territorial strongholds and binding demons and rebuking Satan. They have created a world of demon encounters that is defined not by the Bible but by demon activity itself, forgetting that the Bible says demons deceive and distort the truth.

As mentioned in an earlier chapter, numerous beliefs that many Christians have about demons were fashioned by Frank Peretti's fiction *This Present Darkness*. In this book he wrote about the religious fight against territorial spirits mobilized to dominate a small town.

Some believers have abandoned classic evangelism and disciplined living and are claiming to regain neighborhoods and cities and even countries with prayer walks and deliverance incantations. Many have accepted fiction as fact, led primarily by the writings and influence of Fuller Seminary professor Peter Wagner, who has led "summit" meetings for "cosmic level spiritual warfare."

Certainly the believer is involved in a struggle against the powers of darkness, as Ephesians 6 tells us. However, many of the practices of today's spiritual warfare movement are unfounded and speculative, instead of being grounded in biblical theology.

Are we to learn techniques for casting out demons? Do we deliver incantations against Satan? Can we bind Satan and his fallen angels? If so, for how long are they bound? And if we bind Satan, does that mean he cannot come against us? Is he bound only in our life and no other? Are we to break strongholds of territorial demons and regain cities and countries?

Let's go back to the Bible for this study on **angels, demons, and other flying creatures** and build our understanding of the fallen angels around what the Scriptures actually *say*.

Does Satan Really Exist?

Let's begin by asking and answering the question, "Is the materialist wrong?" Or to put it another way, "Does Satan *really* exist?"

The answer is undeniably **YES!**

Old Testament Evidence

The Old Testament evidence alone is conclusive.

Texts such as Genesis 3:1 and Ezekiel 28:13 confirm that Satan was in the Garden of Eden. These are validated in the New Testament where Paul writes:

> *But I am afraid that, as the serpent deceived Eve by his craftiness, your minds will be led astray from the simplicity and purity of devotion to Christ* (2 Corinthians 11:3).

An Old Testament proof text is:

> *Now there was a day when the sons of God came to present themselves before the LORD, and Satan also came among them. The LORD said to Satan, "From where do you come?" Then Satan answered the LORD and said, "From roaming about on the earth and walking around on it"* (Job 1:6-7).

Furthermore, the Bible says:

> *Then Satan stood up against Israel and moved David to number Israel* (1 Chronicles 21:1).

Also:

> *Then he showed me Joshua the high priest standing before the angel of the LORD, and Satan standing at his right hand to accuse him. The LORD said to Satan, "The LORD rebuke you, Satan! Indeed, the LORD who has chosen Jerusalem rebuke you!"* (Zechariah 3:1-2*a*).

If Satan is a mere force of evil, then you would have to say that the Lord is a mere force of good, that Joshua was not really a person, and that Jerusalem is a make-believe city.

New Testament Evidence

The evidence mounts dramatically in the New Testament. **Nineteen** New Testament books mention Satan by at least one of his many names. Jesus Christ, Himself, referred to Satan's existence **twenty-five** different times.

So, Who Is Satan?

We will look at four insights from Ezekiel 28.

Satan Was Created with the Other Angels

The Lord led Ezekiel to address a king as the one to be judged, but clearly the power behind this king was Satan, and the speech clearly reveals attributes and characteristics of Satan himself:

> *"Son of man, take up a lamentation over the king of Tyre, and say to him, 'Thus says the Lord GOD, You had the seal of perfection, full of wisdom and perfect in beauty. You were in Eden, the garden of God; every precious stone was your covering: the ruby, the topaz and the diamond; the beryl, the onyx, and the jasper; the lapis lazuli, the turquoise, and the emerald; and the gold, the workmanship of your settings and sockets, was in you. On the day that you were created they were prepared'"* (Ezekiel 28:12-13).

This verse clearly teaches the origin of Satan. He was created with all the other angelic hosts sometime before Creation, and then fell sometime before the Fall of Man.

Satan Was Created a Member of the Cherubim

We think of cherubs as fat little baby angels, but a **cherub** is one from among the class of angels known as the **cherubim**:

> *"You were the anointed cherub who covers, and I placed you there. You were on the holy mountain of God; you walked in the midst of the stones of fire. You were blameless in your ways from the day you were created until unrighteousness was found in you"* (Ezekiel 28:14-15).

Satan was evidently created as a member of the class of heavenly beings known as **cherubim**. These were the angels, so to speak, who stood closest to God's throne.

In fact, when the Ark of the Covenant was built, it was constructed with two sculpted **cherubim** on either side of the lid (also called the mercy seat - *Exodus 25*). It was between these two **cherubim** that the glory of God hovered.

Cherubim, armed with a flaming sword, were the ones chosen to guard the Garden of Eden as Adam and Eve were sent out (*Genesis 3*).

When Solomon built the temple, the workers carved the design of **cherubim** into walls and doors (*1 Kings 6*).

These beings were created with four wings and four faces, forming a square and facing each direction: north, south, east, and west. They are able to fly in any direction without ever having to turn around. Their four faces, according to Ezekiel 1, were a man, a lion, a bull, and an eagle.

Now we know from other passages that angel beings had the ability to change their appearance. Some people saw them as "men," such as in the story of Sodom and Gomorrah (*Genesis 19*). Others saw flaming white creatures that seemed to flash like lightning (*Matthew 28*).

There are many things about **angels**, **cherubim**, and **seraphim** that we are not told, and much of what we know, we cannot comprehend.

However, something interesting is divulged about Lucifer. The Bible says that **Satan** is a fallen **cherub** who is able, evidently, to change his appearance, yet created with four faces and four wings. He is a bright creature of beauty, yet exceptionally capable of masquerading with incredible deception.

Satan Was the Highest-Ranking Cherub in Heaven

"By the abundance of your trade you were internally filled with violence, and you sinned; therefore I have cast you as profane from the mountain of God. And I have destroyed you, O covering cherub, from the midst of the stones of fire" (Ezekiel 28:16).

The word "anointed" from verse 14 and this description in verse 16 of the **covering cherub** indicate that before Lucifer fell, he was the highest stationed guardian for God. In verses 12 and 13, we are told that he "had the seal of perfection, full of wisdom and perfect in beauty."

In the New Testament, Satan is considered the highest ranking leader among the fallen angels. In fact, in Matthew 25:41, the demons are actually called *his* angels.

Satan Lost His Position by Sinning against God

People ask, "Why would God create Satan, when He knew Satan would become the enemy?"

For that matter, why allow Judas to be born, knowing Satan would inhabit him and he would betray the Savior?

God created them for the same reason He allows everyone who rejects and hates Him to be born into the world: He gives mankind, as He gave the angels, **self-determination**. That is the ability, from our perspective and will, to choose.

God did not create robots—*that* would have been unloving. He created angels and humans with the ability to exercise obedience toward Him and submission to His will.

> *"Your heart was lifted up because of your beauty; you corrupted your wisdom by reason of your splendor. I cast you to the ground; I put you before kings, that they may see you"* (Ezekiel 28:17).

Satan Possesses Three Personality Traits

1. Intellect

Ezekiel informs us, as did Paul, that he had incredible wisdom and was able to intellectually deceive:

> *But, I am afraid that, as the serpent deceived Eve by his craftiness . . .* (2 Corinthians 11:3*a*).

Then, in the latter part of that verse, Paul warns believers not to allow *your minds* [to] *be led astray* [by Satan] *from the simplicity and purity of devotion to Christ* (2 Corinthians 11:3*b*).

Also, we are reminded by Christ: *"I will build My church; and the gates of hell shall not prevail against it"* (Matthew 16:18*b* KJV).

The anger, hatred, and bitterness of Satan against Christ and His Church is profound.

2. Emotion

Be of sober spirit, be on the alert. Your adversary, the devil, prowls about like a roaring lion, seeking someone to devour (1 Peter 5:8).

It's difficult to imagine the intensity of Satan's hatred toward Christ and His Church.

3. Will

"How you have fallen from heaven, O star of the morning, son of the dawn! You have been cut down to the earth, you who have weakened the nations! But you said in your heart, 'I will ascend to heaven; I will raise my throne above the stars of God, and I will sit on the mount of assembly in the recesses of the north. I will ascend above the heights of the clouds; I will make myself like the Most High.' Nevertheless you will be thrust down to Sheol, to the recesses of the pit" (Isaiah 14:12-15).

"I will . . . I will . . . I will . . . I will . . . I will," this cherub said again and again. Indeed, he was created with a will!

What Are Satan's Names?

There are at least **twenty-one names** of this enemy of Christ and His Church.

Names Depicting Satan's Position

- **Anointed cherub** (*Ezekiel 28:14*)
- **Prince of this world** (*John 12:31, 16:11*)

  The word "world" is the Greek word *kosmos*, which can be translated "ordered system; kingdom." Satan attempts to be like God and thus, he orders and arranges his followers and rules over all who, like him, rebel against God. He is the prince over the fallen cosmos.

- **Prince of the power of the air** (*Ephesians 2:2*)

  You could render this "the ruler of the empire of the atmosphere." It is simply a phrase that conveys his leadership over fallen angels as well as fallen men.

- **The god of this world** (*2 Corinthians 4:4*)

  The word for world in this passage is not *kosmos*, but *aion*. The emphasis of this word is on a system of philosophy or thinking which is self-centered. It refers to the religions of this world which are counterfeit and deceptive. The world may think they worship Buddha, Allah, the Jesus of Mormonism, or the Krishna of the Baghavad Gita but they, in fact, have been deceived. The god they follow is the god of this world—Satan himself.

- **Ruler of the demons** (*Luke 11:15*)

- **Beelzebul** or **lord of the flies** (*Matthew 12:27*)

  Beelzebul is a term that means lord of the flies, which refers to corruption and decay. The word finds its origin in Canaanite idolatry, in which Baal was the chief god. You can only imagine the blasphemy of the Jewish leaders who on one occasion said that Jesus worked through the power of Baal, or Beelzebul (*Matthew 12, Mark 3, Luke 11*).

  These are the names that speak of Satan's position of power.

Names Describing Satan's Disposition

- **Lucifer** (*Isaiah 14:12* KJV)

  This was his original name and it refers to his aura of splendid light.

- **Satan** (many references, e.g., *Luke 22:31*)

  This name simply means "adversary; opposer."

- **The devil** (many references, e.g., *Matthew 4:1*)

  This name is commonly used by Christ and means "slanderer; accuser." The devil accuses the believer before God, and accuses God before the believer.

- **The red dragon** (*Revelation 12:3,4*)

  This is a lesser-known title. It is a term that describes his disposition for bloodshed and violence, his penchant for war, and his lust for killing.

- **The evil one** (*1 John 2:13*).

- **Apollyon** (Greek; *Revelation 9:11*) or **Abaddon** (Hebrew;

Job 26:6, 28:22, 31:12; Psalm 88:11; Proverbs 15:11, 27:20).

These names refer to Satan's relationship with the dead and are the names that describe his disposition.

Names Describing Satan's Imposition

Webster defines one who imposes on another as one who deceives or takes advantage. There are many names of Satan which describe his imposition, that is, his deceiving methods and destructive ways.

- **The tempter** (*1 Thessalonians 3:5*)

  Lest everyone blame temptation on the devil, may I remind you that he is not omnipresent. The Bible tells us in Job 1 that Satan went in and out of the presence of God. The Bible also encourages the Christian that drawing near to God is enough to cause the devil to flee (*James 4:7-8*)! In other words, he cannot personally be tempting one person in California and at the same time, tempting another believer in North Carolina. From the looks of it, he spends a lot of time in Washington, DC, which is all the more reason to pray. He will be where he can influence the most.

  We speak of Hitler's bombing Great Britain, though Hitler never actually piloted the planes and dropped bombs on London. He was behind it though, so we refer to the Blitz as if Hitler himself did it. In that sense the devil, as the leader of the demon world, is said to be behind all demonic temptation.

- **The accuser** (*Revelation 12:10*)
- **The deceiver** (*Revelation 12:9*)
- **The enemy** (*Matthew 13:39*)
- **The father of lies** (*John 8:44*)
- **Murderer** (*John 8:44*)

  This is a powerful combination of titles. He lies to people, they are deceived, and then they die.

Someone sent me a parable which highlights the deception of Satan. This parable could never take place; it's theologically distorted and not to be interpreted literally, or even figuratively. It does illustrate the point of deception in a rather interesting way, though:

There was a sales representative for a marketing agency who was hit by a bus and killed. His soul arrived in heaven, where he went through a series of interviews and finally arrived at the pearly gates. Peter was standing there (in all of these stories, of course, Peter never gets to enjoy heaven because he is always standing at the gate! *Peter said, "Listen, before you get settled in, it seems we have a problem. You see, we've never once had anyone in advertising make it this far. We're not sure you really know what you're doing here. So we have higher orders to have you make a choice. We're going to require that you spend some time in hell and some time in heaven and then, you can decide where you'd rather be."The salesman said, "That won't be necessary, I'd much prefer heaven." "Sorry," Peter said, "that's the way it is for you."*

With that, Peter put the man in an elevator that went straight down to hell. The doors opened and the man found himself stepping out onto the putting green of a beautiful golf course. In the distance was a country club, and standing in front of him were all of his old friends from the firm. They were dressed in tuxedos and had beautiful women on their arms. They were cheering for him and welcoming him to hell. (By the way, I have actually had several people tell me they would rather be in hell with their friends than in heaven.) *They ran up, slapped him on the back, and talked about old times. They promised a round of golf on the next day and went into the country club where they enjoyed a dinner of steak and lobster. A demon even came over and offered him a Cuban cigar. Before he knew it, it was time to leave. Everybody shook his hand, waved goodbye, and said, "Please come back and stay."*

The elevator went up . . . up . . . up, and there was Peter waiting for him. He said, "Okay, now it's time for a day in heaven." The man replied, "Never mind, I've already decided. I'd like to live in hell." Peter said, "Are you absolutely sure?" "Yes sir," the man said.

So, back in the elevator and down went the salesman. When the doors opened, he found himself standing in a desolate wasteland. The heat was unbearable and moaning and crying could be heard all around him. The devil came up to him and said, "So, you've decided." "Yes, but I don't understand. A few hours ago, I was here and there was a golf course and a country club and lobster, but now, this is torment; it's miserable. Why is it so different?" The devil looked at him, smiled, and said, "A few hours ago, you were a prospect. Now, you're a client."

Isn't that so true? The prospect of sin is so alluring—it promises so much, but its deception is an evil mirage.

- **The adversary** (*1 Peter 5:8*)

  In 1 Peter 5:8, Satan is pictured as a roaring lion seeking someone to devour. This is a serious warning to the believer. The word "devour" means "to discredit; to ruin; to destroy."

- **That old serpent** (*Revelation 12:9*)

  I found it interesting that in the first book of the Bible, we are introduced to Satan as a serpent, and in the last book of the Bible, he is referred to as that old serpent.

- **The angel of light** (*2 Corinthians 11:14*)

It is abundantly clear that Satan does exist and that every reference to him is a reference to a being who loves himself, hates God, and despises all who follow the risen Lord!

Five Things to Remember

1. The power of Satan is delegated.
2. The influence of Satan is limited.
3. The success of Satan is permitted.
4. The judgment of Satan is determined.
5. **The destruction of Satan's kingdom is guaranteed.**

Make no mistake, while Satan's power, influence, and success are avoidable and can be eluded by the obedient believer, and although his judgment and destruction are already determined and guaranteed, he is still at this moment influencing the **world**. And far too often, the **world** is influencing the **believer**.

The following is fictitious . . . but thought-provoking:
*Satan called a world-wide convention. In his opening address to his evil angels, he said, "We can't keep Christians from going to church; we can't keep them from reading their Bibles and knowing the truth; we can't even keep Christians from forming intimate, abiding relationships with Christ (**once they gain this connection with Christ,***

our power over them is broken). So, let them go to their churches; let them have their conservative lifestyles, but let's steal their time so they can't gain that close relationship with Christ. This is what I, Satan, want you to do. Distract them from maintaining closeness with Christ."

"How shall we do this?" shouted his fallen angels. He replied, "Keep them busy in the non-essentials of life and invent innumerable schemes to occupy their minds. Tempt them to spend, spend, spend, and borrow, borrow, borrow. Persuade the wives to go to work for long hours and the husbands to work six or seven days each week, ten to twelve hours a day, so they can afford their empty lifestyles. Keep them from spending time with their children, and as their family fragments, soon their home will offer no escape from the pressures of life."

He continued, "Over-stimulate their minds, so they cannot hear that still, small voice. Entice them to play their radio whenever they drive and to keep the TV, DVDs, CDs, and PCs going constantly in their home. See to it that every store and restaurant in the world plays non-biblical music incessantly. This will jam their minds and break sweet fellowship with Christ. Fill the coffee tables with magazines and newspapers; pound their minds with the news twenty-four hours a day; invade their driving moments with billboards; flood their mailboxes with junk mail, catalogues, sweepstakes, and every kind of newsletter and promotional that offers free products, services, and false hopes. Splash the pictures of models and celebrities on magazine covers so the husbands will believe that external beauty is what is important, and they'll become dissatisfied with life. That will frag-ment those families quickly."

He added, "Even in their recreation, let them be excessive. Have them return from their recreation exhausted, disquieted, and unprepared for the coming week. Don't let them reflect on God's wonders; send them to amusement parks, sporting events, concerts, and movies instead. Keep them busy, busy, busy. And when they meet for spiritual fellowship, involve them in gossip and small talk, so they leave with troubled consciences and unsettled emotions. Let them be involved in winning souls, but crowd their lives with so many good causes they have no time to seek after the Lord."

"This will work!" the fallen angels cried. It was quite a convention. The evil angels went eagerly to their assignments, causing Christians everywhere to become busier and more rushed, going here and there.

My friend, while Satan cannot **destroy** the believer, he can **distract** the believer. So this week, be on guard! Be alert and aware as you walk with Christ.

THE FALLEN CHERUB

Digging Deeper:

But I am afraid that, as the serpent deceived Eve by his craftiness, your minds will be led astray from the simplicity and purity of devotion to Christ (2 Corinthians 11:3).

This text teaches that our mind has the potential of being led astray from devotion to Christ by the deception of Satan. The devil would love nothing more than to see a beloved child of God become **distracted with good things** such as doctrine and ministry, and in doing so, lose sight of the simplicity of Christian obedience (which is simply loving God and loving others.)

If our **theology** (the truth about God) is not followed by our **doxology** (worship of God), then our **ministry** is worthless and our **mind** has been deceived by the devil.

Read Revelation 2:1-7 and notice how Satan deceived the church at Ephesus into losing their simple and pure devotion to Christ.

The most important thing was lacking: loving Christ.

List some of the good things about this church that were actually diversions from the best thing:

_____

_____

_____

_____

"You were the anointed cherub who covers, and I placed you there. You were on the holy mountain of God; you walked in the midst of the stones of fire. You were blameless in your ways from the day you were created until unrighteousness was found in you" (Ezekiel 28:14-15).

In this description, what was Satan like before his fall?

_____

_____

_____

"But you said in your heart, 'I will ascend to heaven; I will raise my throne above the stars of God, and I will sit on the mount of assembly in the recesses of the north. I will ascend above the heights of the clouds; I will make myself like the Most High'" (Isaiah 14:13-14).

Satan obviously had a little something called a **pride** issue. Circle each time he uses the phrase "I will" in this passage (these are references to his own ambitious goals).

Read the passage again and notice how Satan never actually said these words with his mouth but merely thought them in his heart! Because God hates pride so much and cannot tolerate even the thought of it (*Proverbs 6:16-19*), Satan's heavenly citizenship was forever cut off, due to his prideful heart.

Have you ever stopped to think that maybe Christians have more in common with the devil than we thought? Be honest; have you ever thought in your heart that your way was somehow better than God's but you were too afraid to say it to His face? What about your will at this moment?

Do you have thoughts that, up until now, you've deceived yourself into believing that God doesn't know? If so, in what areas of your life are you, like Satan, saying to yourself, "I will!" instead of, "Lord, if You will"?

First, pray for God to reveal the pride that you have been excusing and circle any of the examples listed above that directly apply to your heart.

Write down additional struggles in this area that you are currently "demanding from God."

_____

_____

_____

_____

[I]n whose case the god of this world has blinded the minds of the unbelieving so that they might not see the light of the gospel of the glory of Christ, who is the image of God (2 Corinthians 4:4).

Would you agree that Satan usually receives more credit than he deserves? In other words, we like to deny our own responsibility by blaming him for our sinful behavior.

Are we really as helpless and vulnerable as we say we are, or do we simply play the same old blame game that Adam and Eve played in the very beginning of time (*Genesis 3:12-13*)?

When 2 Corinthians 4:4 says that Satan is the "god of this world," does that mean he has the power to dictate our choices?

___ Yes!

___ I think so!

___ No, because _____

If Satan is the "god of this world," does sinning become inevitable and is holiness an impossible way to live? Read James 1:12-15 before pondering these questions, and then write your answer.

_____
_____
_____
_____
_____

Take It to Heart:
Just how busy are you?

Name four ways that Satan loves to try to distract you from the simplicity of devotion to Christ on a daily basis:

1._____
2._____
3._____
4._____

List four specific actions that you will take in order to rid yourself of these distractions. Don't write anything down if you don't plan on doing anything about it!

1._____
2._____
3._____
4._____

Unmasking the Serpent

A Snake in the Grass

The fall of the Russian monarchy occurred July 16, 1918; the last czar of Russia, Nicholas II, and his wife and children were executed by the Bolsheviks. That was over ninety years ago.

If I were to ask you what the single most important factor in the downfall of a thousand-year-old Russian monarchy was, the murders of Czar Nicholas II and his family, plus the rise of Vladimir Lenin and Russian communism would be good answers. If I asked what the fundamental cause was that prepared the way for the above, you would probably never imagine that the answer would be the work of one demonically empowered man named Grigory Yefimovich.

While Grigory was still in his teens, he gained a reputation for two things: being able to somewhat predict the future, and living an immoral lifestyle. The local villagers gave him the nickname Rasputin, which means "debauchery." When he was twenty-two, he made a spiritual pilgrimage to Mount Athos in Greece. There he came under the influence of a heretical religious sect known as the Flagelents. They believed sinning was necessary to salvation—the more you sinned, the more secure your salvation. Two years later Rasputin reappeared in his Russian village as a mysterious holy man with a penchant for immorality and an unusual ability to cure the sick.

Rasputin eventually wandered into the capital city of St. Petersburg, where society was in the midst of delving into mysticism and the occult. They warmly received this "priest" who had already gained a modest reputation as a faith healer. Rasputin gained an audience with the imperial family of Czar Nicholas and his wife Alexandra. They were struggling with the incurable condition of their son, who suffered from hemophilia. Through hypnosis, Rasputin was able to alleviate the suffering of their son. Because of that, he was welcomed into the family circle as a close and trusted friend. Alexandra came to revere him as a holy man sent by God to save her son and her husband's throne.

Under the spell of his influence as chief advisor, however, capable men were exiled and corrupt men put in their place. Even after Alexandra was confronted with Rasputin's immoral and financial scandals in and out of court, she refused to act on any of it. She was strangely protective of this holy man who had power to help her son.

When World War I broke out, Czar Nicholas took personal command of the army, leaving Alexandra and Rasputin even greater power than ever before. Key leaders were exiled at Rasputin's wish and the economy and public morale plummeted to the bottom. Strikes and riots erupted in the capital city and rumors began to circulate about the relationship between Rasputin and Alexandra.

A group in the cabinet and members of the royal family secretly conspired to kill Rasputin. On the night of December 30, 1916, Rasputin was invited to what he thought to be a royal party. Instead, he was given poisoned wine, was shot when he tried to escape, and was thrown into a river, where he drowned.

However, the damage to the Russian nation had already been done. Evil men were still in power, and the czar and Alexandra both lost all credibility. In March of the following year, Czar Nicholas was forced to abdicate his throne. Approximately a year later, he and his family were brutally murdered by the Russian rebels called Bolsheviks. The vacuum of leadership was filled by the leader of these rebels, whose nickname was Lenin. He brought with him his new ideas of Russian communism.

What was behind the fall of that Russian monarchy? A demonically empowered man with evil ambitions.

One historian wrote, "If there had been no Rasputin, there never would have been a Lenin—no Lenin, and there never would have been the propagation of atheistic communism through the empire of the Soviet Union."

A false spiritual leader—a supposed holy man, empowered by the kingdom of darkness with the power to heal—deceived the royal family and ultimately opened the way for almost a century of atheistic communism to dominate nearly one billion people.

There is little doubt in my mind that Satan is a mastermind, determined to influence and deceive nations. He often does so through single individuals like Rasputin.

But how does Satan impact the life of an individual who is a believer? Can a Christian be demon possessed? Furthermore, what power does the demonic world have over the Church at large and the believer in particular?

Let's answer these questions, not by explaining **stories** but by the exegesis of the **Scriptures**.

Three different words are used in the Bible to refer to Satan's specific operation against the believer. Let's look at these.

Satan's Three Strategies against Believers

The Schemes of Satan

For to this end also I wrote that I might put you to the test, whether you are obedient in all things. But one whom you forgive anything, I forgive also; for indeed what I have forgiven, if I have forgiven anything, I did it for your sakes in the presence of Christ, so that no advantage be taken of us by Satan; for we are not ignorant of his **schemes** (2 Corinthians 2:9-11).

As we unmask the serpent and reveal not only his true nature but his ways, his approaches, his patterns, his plotting against the believer, we discover the interesting word **schemes**. Paul warns the believer of the **schemes** of Satan.

The Greek word is *noema*, which refers to the intellectual activity of the mind. It can be rendered "purposes; plans" of the mind. In a sinister way, as it relates to Satan, it can refer to evil plots and devices, or literally, **evil scheming**.

It appears again several chapters later where the word **speculations** also comes from the Greek word *noema*:

We are destroying **speculations** *and every lofty thing raised up against the knowledge of God, and we are taking every thought captive to the obedience of Christ* (2 Corinthians 10:5).

This verse and verses 3 and 4 have produced a number of fanciful theological interpretations within the modern spiritual warfare movement. Many people visualize the believer with a lance, riding a horse, sounding a battle cry, and crashing the castle walls of demonic strongholds to the ground.

In verse 4, ***divinely powerful for the destruction of fortresses*** is a reference to that which a person relies upon intellectually or the reasoning that an unbeliever hides behind. Many biblical scholars believe that Paul was referring to this verse in which the same Greek word for fortress appears in the Septuagint (the Greek translation of the Hebrew Bible):

> *A wise man . . . **brings down the stronghold** [fortress] **in which they trust*** (Proverbs 21:22).

Therefore, the fortress is a metaphor for ungodly intellectual reasoning. It is not some mystical castle inhabited by demons but, rather, scholarly cerebral arguments that Satan has used to intellectually deceive the unbeliever.

Can we be sure that Paul is referring to mental defenses in the minds of unbelievers, motivated and encouraged by Satan and his demons? Do we really know that these fortresses are not a reference to territorial strongholds that need to be crushed by cosmic warfare?

Yes; all we have to do is read the next verse. The Bible has a way of explaining itself. Remember this principle: **All the Bible is a commentary on any one verse of the Bible.** So, the more you refer to the Bible in all of its verses, the better you will understand the Bible in any one of its verses.

Paul describes the fortresses of human intellect that are being destroyed by the truth:

> *We are destroying speculations and every lofty thing . . . and we are taking every* **thought** *captive to the obedience of Christ* (2 Corinthians 10:5).

Speculations or *logismos* in the Greek means "worldly logic; worldly reasoning."

Lofty thing means to lift up one's self and is a metaphor to the erecting of a tower of human pride and self sufficiency.

Paul uses a present tense verb "taking every thought captive." He is saying that we constantly capture and bring into captivity every anti-God thought. This indicates the ongoing daily war within the mind.

If we want to know how to daily battle the mental **schemes** of Satan, who seeks to trouble, deceive, harass, and rob the peace and assurance of the believer, here's the plan to follow:

> *Finally, brethren, whatever is true, whatever is honorable, whatever is right, whatever is pure, whatever is lovely, whatever is of good repute, if there is any excellence and if anything worthy of praise, let your mind dwell on these things. The things you have learned and received and heard and seen in me, practice these things; and the God of peace shall be with you* (Philippians 4:8-9).

Most believers would never admit that Satan has captured their minds with his **schemes**, but how many would say that the state of their mind and spirit is characterized by peace? Would you describe your mind and your life in general with words like **serenity** or **contentment**?

If not, the discipline of Philippians 4:8-9 asks the questions, "Were the television and movies you watched this past week pure and true? Were the things you read excellent and honorable? Were the conversations you had, the relationships and friendships you participated in right and of godly reputation? Did you practice these things and feel the peace of God?"

The Systems of Satan

> *Put on the full armor of God, so that you will be able to stand firm against the* **schemes** *of the devil. For our struggle is not against flesh and blood, but against the rulers, against the powers, against the world forces of this darkness, against the spiritual forces of wickedness in the heavenly places. Therefore, take up the full armor of God, that you may be able to resist in the evil day, and having done everything, to stand firm* (Ephesians 6:11-13).

This word is different from the Greek word we looked at earlier, even though it is translated **schemes**. The Greek word in Ephesians is *methodias*, which gives us our transliterated word **methods**.

We are to clothe ourselves in the armor of God, which will enable us to withstand the **methods** and **systems** of Satan.

I remember my older brother and I, along with a neighborhood kid or two, going to a particular neighbor's house on occasion. It had a yard that bordered a two-lane street with regular traffic traveling thirty-five miles an hour. In that yard was a row of hedges about waist high, bordering the road and running the distance of the side yard. Those bushes provided the perfect ambush spot. We would store our peaches and wait for a car to drive by. Just as a car came past us, we would jump up and let our peaches fly. Sometimes we would hear the gratifying thump and know that some ripe peach just splattered the target. Sometimes the car would screech to a halt, and we would hear, "Hey you . . ." We would race to the other side of the yard, dive headfirst over another row of hedges, and make our escape. We loved peach season!

*Now, to those drivers, what we did was irritating, probably startling, and it created a messy spot that they had to clean up when they got home. It was **just** peaches to the mischievous boys who planned the attacks.*

Most Christians seem to think that Satan is just some mischievous little man who lobs peaches at us every once in a while as we drive through life. We think he is not too organized, doesn't have very good aim, and only intends to startle us or make a little mess of things when he has the chance. He's not much worse than a ripe peach in the wrong place.

To the contrary! Peter wrote:

[T]*he devil, prowls about like a roaring lion, seeking someone to devour* (1 Peter 5:8).

The word **devour** could be translated "discredit; ruin; destroy."

We're not given specifics in Ephesians 6 as to what the **methods** are by which Satan devours and destroys. However, the word *methodias* appears earlier in the book:

And He gave some as apostles, and some as prophets, and some as evangelists, and some as pastors and teachers, for the equipping of the saints for the work of service, to the building up of the body of Christ; until we all attain to the unity of the faith, and of the knowledge of the Son of God, to a mature man, to the measure of the stature which belongs to the fullness of Christ. As a result, we are no longer to be children, tossed here and

there by waves and carried about by every wind of doctrine, by the trickery of men, by craftiness in deceitful scheming; but speaking the truth in love, we are to grow up in all aspects into Him who is the head, even Christ (Ephesians 4:11-15).

You could translate it "by crafty methods of deception." Once again, the primary attack of Satan is upon the mind of the believer.

The deceptive lies of Satan continually buffet the believer, whether they are communicated through the media or the pride of our own sinful nature. It could be through the temptations of the flesh or the philosophy of a greedy world system. The battle is real; it is deadly serious; it is daily.

I am convinced that every believer encounters one of Satan's methods every day. Call it a daily test of integrity, purity, purpose, or honesty—you name it. Every day you face a test.

Four Tests in Satan's System Used against the Believer

1. **Temptation** – an attempt to discredit the believer and destroy fellowship with God.

2. **Persecution** – an attempt to discourage the believer and damage trust in God.

3. **Division** – an attempt to disrupt the community of believers and dissolve unity with others.

4. **Deception** – an attempt to distract the believer and dilute the purity of the Gospel.

In other words, Satan is not lobbing ripe little peaches at us. What we have to lose is not just time cleaning up peach stains. It is a matter of:

- upholding God's reputation;
- being Christ's glory and honor in the world;
- being usable by Christ for the advancement of His Church;
- enjoying the preciousness of unity;
- protecting the purity of the Gospel.

The **systems** of Satan are designed to destroy all of these, if they can. He is ruthless. He is patient. He is organized. He is cunning. He is proficient.

The Snares of Satan

There is another word that is found in 1 Timothy that further unmasks this enemy and reveals another nuance of his ways. There are the **schemes** of Satan, the **systems** of Satan, and there are also the **snares** of Satan. Paul demands that elders in the Church meet certain qualifications:

> [A]*nd not a new convert, so he will not become conceited and fall into the condemnation incurred by the devil. And he must have a good reputation with those outside the church, so that he may not fall into reproach and the* **snare** *of the devil* (1 Timothy 3:6-7).

Paul uses the same word to describe the unbeliever who is caught up in the **snare** of Satan:

> *The Lord's bond-servant must not be quarrelsome, but be kind to all, able to teach, patient when wronged, with gentleness correcting those who are in opposition, if perhaps God may grant them repentance leading to the knowledge of the truth, and they may come to their senses and escape from the* **snare** *of the devil, having been held captive by him to do his will* (2 Timothy 2:24-26).

Paul uses that word to refer to a believer who, by pride, falls into the **snare** of the devil and loses his credibility. He uses the very same word to refer to an unbeliever who is totally caught up by the **snare** of the devil.

Can Christians Be Possessed by Demons?

We know that unbelievers can actually be possessed by demons who have ensnared them. So, can a believer also be possessed or inhabited by demonic spirits?

Many proponents of the modern-day warfare movement say yes. They point to deliverance ministries that rescue believers from all sorts of demons: cancer, poverty, alcohol, laziness, etc.

They, however, have no biblical ground to stand on. Furthermore, they do not understand what Paul wrote:

> *For He* [God] *rescued us from the domain of darkness, and transferred us to the kingdom of His beloved Son* (Colossians 1:13).

Our redemption frees us from any claim of Satan: [We have been] *called . . . out of darkness into His marvelous light* (1 Peter 2:9).

Those who believe they can be owned by God yet demonized do not draw on Scripture for their belief in this regard. They are relying on subjective experiences and stories that have made the rounds. Nowhere in the New Testament is there an illustration of a believer who is inhabited by a demon.

One author wrote (and I wholeheartedly agree):

There is no example in the Bible where a demon ever inhabited or invaded a true believer. Never in the New Testament epistles are believers warned about the possibility of being inhabited by demons. Neither do we see believers rebuking, binding, or casting demons out of a true believer. The epistles never instruct believers to cast out demons, whether from a believer or unbeliever. Christ and the apostles were the only ones who cast out demons (as a sign, I might add, of Christ's credentials as the Son of God), and in every instance the demon-possessed person was an unbeliever.[5]

Certainly there is conflict with the enemy—we are talking about the serpent's **schemes** and **snares**. But we need to understand that this is vastly different from believing that demons can spatially inhabit a believer.

Charles Ryrie is a highly respected author and theologian. He gave this definition regarding demon possession, and it is consistent with what we read in the entire New Testament record:

[It is] *a demon residing in a person, exerting direct control and influence over that person, with certain derangement of mind and/or body. Demon possession is to be distinguished from demon influence or activity in relation to a person. The work of the demon in the latter is from the outside; in demon possession, it is from within.*[6]

These two statements summarize the definition:

- While the enemy can **influence** the believer, he cannot **possess** the believer.

- While the enemy cannot **possess** the believer, he can **destroy** the believer.

I believe this clears up the issue.

People Impacted by Satan for God's Purpose

Now, for the remaining part of our discussion on unmasking the serpent, let's look at illustrations in the Bible of both believer and unbeliever who were impacted by Satan, and see what we learn from them.

Paul: To Ensure Personal Humility

The Apostle Paul struggled with pride and God used Satan as an agent of His sovereign purpose. He wrote:

> *Because of the surpassing greatness of the revelations, for this reason, to keep me from exalting myself, there was given to me a thorn in the flesh, a messenger of Satan to buffet me— to keep me from exalting myself* (2 Corinthians 12:7)*!*

Many people have tried to identify Paul's thorn (epilepsy, poor eyesight, malaria?), but we are not told what it was. The Greek word for "buffet" refers to bone-crushing blows. Whatever it was, it hurt; it distracted him; it plagued him.

Nowhere do we read that Paul attempted to bind, rebuke, or cast out this Satanic messenger. Paul simply prayed that God would remove the thorn, and God chose not to answer Paul's prayer in the way Paul wanted:

> *Therefore I am well content with weaknesses, with insults, with distresses, with persecutions, with difficulties, for Christ's sake* . . . (2 Corinthians 12:10).

If Paul were living today he would never be interviewed on *The 700 Club*. In the eyes of modern Christianity, Paul would be a loser. People would say, "What do you mean you're content with distresses and difficulties?"

People today would be giving Paul *The Prayer of Jabez* and saying, "Listen, Paul, what you need to do is pray that prayer—you're not receiving God's blessings."

No. Satan was allowed access into Paul's life to ensure personal humility, and Paul received the greater blessing:

> *And He* [God] . . . *said to me, "My grace is sufficient for you, for power is perfected in weakness"* (2 Corinthians 12:9).

Peter: To Develop Spiritual Maturity

Satan was allowed access into the life of Peter in order to develop spiritual maturity.

Jesus said to Peter:

Simon, Simon [Peter]**, behold, Satan has demanded permission to sift you like wheat** (Luke 22:31).

Then Jesus said, in effect, "But once you've repented, you'll be prepared for effective, lasting ministry."

Judas: To Advance Redemption's Plan and Fulfill Prophecy

Judas was actually inhabited by Satan, thus proving he was an unbeliever—for **the Spirit of God and the serpent of hell will not occupy the same temple**. Satan impacted the life of Judas, but it was the will of God, in order to advance redemption's plan and to fulfill the prophecy that He would be betrayed by one of His own (*John 13:21*).

Church Members: To Maintain Moral and Doctrinal Purity within the Church

There are several biblical illustrations of church members who were influenced by Satan. We do not know if all were believers. However, Satan was allowed to impact their lives in order to maintain moral and doctrinal purity within the church.

We are told that there was a man who persisted in immorality. He was living with his stepmother in an incestuous relationship. The church refused to deal with the man who, evidently, was a believer.

Paul records:

In the name of our Lord Jesus, when you are assembled, and I with you in spirit, with the power of our Lord Jesus, I have decided to deliver such a one to Satan for the destruction of his flesh, that his spirit may be saved in the day of the Lord Jesus (1 Corinthians 5:4-5).

Satan actually causes the death of believers who refuse to repent. He acts as God's agent in bringing discipline to its final stage.

In another letter, Paul uses the same language:

[S]*ome have rejected and suffered shipwreck in regard to their faith. Among these are Hymenaeus and Alexander, whom I have delivered over to Satan, so that they may be taught not to blaspheme* (1 Timothy 1:19-20).

Paul's instruction is a lot different from what we hear today. Rather than delivering people *from* Satan, Paul actually says that the Church sometimes delivers people *to* Satan! Now that is a deliverance ministry few speak about today! That won't sell any books, but it will purify the Church.

In Acts 5:1-11 Ananias and his wife Sapphira brought a gift of money to the apostles, saying it was the money they had earned from the sale of some personal property. Ananias came to the church meeting first.

But Peter said, "Ananias, why has Satan filled your heart to lie to the Holy Spirit and to keep back some of the price of the land? And as he heard those words, Ananias fell down and breathed his last . . . (Acts 5:3, 5).

Then, Sapphira came in:

And Peter responded to her, "Tell me whether you sold the land for such and such a price?" (Acts 5:8).

The remaining members of the congregation must have held their breath as they awaited the answer:

[A]*nd she said, "Yes, that was the price." Then Peter said to her . . . "Behold, the feet of those who have buried your husband are at the door, and they will carry you out as well." And immediately she fell at his feet and breathed her last . . .* (Acts 5:9-10).

The church had its second funeral that day.

This gives the idea that Satan the Destroyer, at any moment when given permission from sovereign God, will shatter a believer's life.

Succeeding Against Satan

How do you avoid Satan's **snares**, **systems**, and **schemes**? These principles are given for the believer who desires to complete his race.

The Principle of Consecration

This is simply allowing the One who **owns** you to **operate** you. Paul wrote:

> [Y]*our body is a temple of the Holy Spirit who is in you, whom you have from God, and . . . you are not your own* (1 Corinthians 6:19).

The principle of consecration merely means that you allow the owner of the vehicle to operate it as He sees fit.

The Principle of Concentration

Where is your focus? Who are you following? Who is influencing you? Who is your teacher and guide?

There are basically two ways of trying to overcome temptation. These are illustrated wonderfully, albeit accidentally, in the Greek myths of Ulysses and Jason. You will understand as you read these myths:

When Ulysses and his men set sail on their journey of conquest, they were warned to avoid the sirens (sea nymphs who by their sweet singing lured mariners to destruction on the rocks surrounding their island) *at all costs. They were told that the sirens' voices were alluring but fatal to all who stopped to listen. The unfortunate listeners became rooted like a tree and could not tear themselves away until they died of hunger. "Fill your companions' ears with wax," he was counseled. "If you yourself want to listen to their songs, first let your men bind you securely to the mast."*

Ulysses heeded the advice. "If the melody beguiles me," he ordered his men, "I charge you, disobey my word, and bend more strongly to your oars."

At length, Ulysses heard the beautiful strains that stole into his mind, overpowered his body, and overcame his will. As the music came sweeter and sweeter, Ulysses' love for home weakened. He struggled with his shame, but at last the bewitching voices of the sirens prevailed. "Loose me and let me stay with the sirens!" he raged. He threatened and entreated; he promised, with desperate signs and gestures, to give his men mountains of gold. They only bound him more securely. He raged and tore at his bonds, for it was agony for him to leave the spot. But not until the last sound of music died away did they loose him. He had passed the zone of temptation.

Jason and his men set out in search of the Golden Fleece. He also was warned of the sirens, and as they sailed, they began to hear the bewitching strains. All around they could see the shore strewn with the bones of those who had succumbed to the sirens' charms. There were seagulls in long lines and shoals of fish that came to listen.

Soon the oars of Jason's men fell from their hypnotized hands. Their heads drooped and their heavy eyes closed. On board was Orpheus, king of minstrels, and he began to sing loudly. He struck his skillful hand over the strings of his harp and his voice rose like a trumpet. The music penetrated the souls of the infatuated men, and their souls thrilled at the sound.

Orpheus continued singing until his voice completely drowned out the voices of the sirens. Once again the men took up their oars, and Jason and his men sailed to victory. "Sing the song again, Orpheus," they cried, "we will dare and suffer to the last." [7]

These two stories strikingly illustrate two ways of handling temptation.

One is to put wax in your ears—escape to a monastery or convent, hide away in a room and never go out into the world. That way, you will never have to hear the sirens' song.

The other is to concentrate on the voice of another—hear the voice and music of heaven as far lovelier and more desirable than the alluring music of earth.

It simply comes down to this: on whose voice are you concentrating?

Consecration and **concentration**: two certain ways to defeat the siren sounds of the serpent!

Unmasking the Serpent

Digging Deeper:

Put on the full armor of God, so that you will be able to stand firm against the schemes of the devil (Ephesians 6:11).

[T]he devil prowls around like a roaring lion, seeking someone to devour (1 Peter 5:8*b*).

The word **devour** in 1 Peter 5:8, means to discredit, ruin, or destroy. Satan is likened to a roaring lion because not only is he the king of this world, he is also the ultimate predator who is constantly on the prowl. Even with this unnerving truth in mind, it is actually possible for Christians to stand firm against this deadly hunter of souls. According to Paul's letter to the Ephesians, what can you do to protect yourself from the jaws of this enemy (*Ephesians 6:11-18*)?

(v. 13) _____

(v. 14) _____

(v. 15) _____

(v. 16) _____

(v. 17) _____

For He [God] *rescued us from the domain of darkness, and transferred us to the kingdom of His beloved Son* (Colossians 1:13).

Since it is impossible for a Christian to be possessed by Satan, is it possible for a Christian to be influenced and led by Satan? Read Colossians 3:1-11 and think critically through your answer. Write your answer below:

_____

_____

_____

_____

Or do you not know that your body is a temple of the Holy Spirit who is in you, whom you have from God, and that you are not your own (1 Corinthians 6:19)?

The principle of consecration is simply defined as allowing the owner of the vehicle to operate it as He sees fit. The principle of concentration focuses a little more on this question, "Who are you allowing to drive your life?"

Remember, even though Satan is no longer the captain of your ship when you become a Christian, he is still barking out orders to you from below deck. It is your choice whether you will listen to the destructive messages of the enemy or the constructive message of your new Captain . . . Jesus Christ.

Conduct a brief internal survey and ask yourself, "Who's voice am I listening to?" Meditate on that question for a few moments and then list some of the areas in your life where you seem to have a hard time surrendering to your Captain.

_____

_____

_____

After you've written down these areas of struggle you are now more aware of in your own life, pray that God will give you the desire, as well as the strength that is necessary, for change to take place.

Write your request in a short prayer here:

Dear Father,

_____

_____

_____

_____

_____

Take It to Heart:

Submit therefore to God. Resist the devil and he will flee from you. Draw near to God and He will draw near to you. Cleanse your hands, you sinners; and purify your hearts, you double-minded. Be miserable and mourn and weep; let your laughter be turned to mourning and your joy to gloom. Humble yourselves in the presence of the Lord, and He will exalt you (James 4:7-10).

You have been asked to identify and list weak areas in your life that the devil would take advantage of and ultimately use in bringing your testimony to ruin. In light of this, as well as the personal struggles you identified earlier, write down some practical ways in which you can avoid temptation that might cause you to stumble in your own life:

_____

_____

_____

_____

_____

You have already asked yourself the questions "What are my problem areas?" and "How can I avoid them?" but this is only the first step. The next step is even more critical; you must ask yourself this very crucial question: "Am I willing to stop sinning in these areas and submit to the Lord?"

Submit therefore to God. Resist the devil and he will flee from you (James 4:7).

As you read this verse, don't ask yourself if you are willing to resist the devil; instead, ask yourself, "Am I willing to submit to God?" Because that's the real battle. Are you ready for the battle of submission?

___ Yes, but not today.

___ Yes, after this one last time.

___ Maybe when I'm older.

___ No, sin feels too good.

Submitting to God is a 24/7/365 battle that requires more strength than you and I could ever have and more faith than you and I care to give. Don't allow yourself to be deceived by the enemy into thinking you have what it takes because it is only through the grace, faithfulness, and absolute power of God that you and I even have a chance of gaining victory over Satan.

If your answer is "Yes, I'm ready to submit today," then you probably noticed that there is no space for this option. The reason for this is because submission is a commitment to God . . . not just a check in the blank on the page. Instead of asking you to put a checkmark on a piece of paper, pray that God will give you a persevering and submissive spirit which will, in turn, allow you to resist the devil today. There is victory in Jesus!!

What to Wear to War

Defining the Battle

I believe that one of the most misunderstood areas within the Christian community at large is the area of spiritual warfare.

On the one hand are those who do not seem to understand that Christianity involves conflict—that the enemy is alive and roaming about, seeking whom he may devour. Most believers do not seem overly convinced that while the advancement of the Church is a promised victory, the gates of hell still mount assaults against it.

On the other hand are those who have come to believe that direct conflict with Satan and demonic forces is at the heart of the Christian life. Confronting, binding, rebuking demons is the ticket, not only for spiritual growth, but for the declaration of the Gospel. So, in order to evangelize one's town, one must first identify and bind the demon of that town.

I recently read that one church-planting pastor just took out a phone book and went street by street, rebuking the controlling neighborhood spirits and asking God's Spirit to bring them to church. He did this instead of canvassing the neighborhoods, meeting people, and inviting them to church.

I guess he was forgetting that not one verse or illustration in the Bible ever tells us that **God will bring the world to the Church**. Not one verse ever tells the **world to go to the Church**. Rather, the church is told to **go and reach the world**.

Jesus tells us to:

"Go into all the world and preach the gospel to all creation" (Mark 16:15).

"[Y]ou shall be My witnesses both in Jerusalem, and in all Judea and Samaria, and even to the remotest part of the earth" (Acts 1:8b).

Charisma is a flagship magazine for the charismatic community which has bought into the contemporary warfare movement hook, line, and sinker. The magazine ran an article a few years ago about a pastor whose church would not grow. He eventually identified the demon of witchcraft who had dominion over that particular geographical area. The pastor began naming the streets around the neighborhood and then commanded the demon to release that territory. The demon complained but finally relented. Since then, the church has grown from seventy to one hundred fifty people.

So-called spiritual warfare advocates claim that it is important to discern the nature of the ruling demons over a city. One author said, "If you know what that demon specializes in, and especially if you know his name, then your prayers will be much more effective."

Spiritual warfare experts have identified the ruling demon of Los Angeles (the home of the film industry) as Pornography. The ruling demon over New York City is Greed, and the ruling demon over Washington, D.C., is Power. Now that they know the names, they can pray against those demons and God's power can be advanced.

That may sound exciting, but what does it imply about the nature of prayer and the sovereignty of God? I don't think God is in heaven saying, "I'll release that neighborhood to your Gospel efforts down there if you can just figure out what the demon's name is. If you can't, sorry—my hands are tied; there's nothing more I can do."

There is not one verse of Scripture that encourages, teaches, exhorts, or directs the New Testament believer to discover territorial demons and bind them.

The primary passage that contemporary warfare advocates say proves the need for such territorial warfare is:

> *In the third year of Cyrus king of Persia a message was revealed to Daniel, who was named Belteshazzar; and the message was true and one of great conflict, but he understood the message and had an understanding of the vision.*
>
> *In those days, I, Daniel, had been mourning for three entire weeks. I did not eat any tasty food, nor did meat or wine enter my mouth, nor did I use any ointment at all until the entire three weeks were completed. On the twenty-fourth day of the first month, while I was by the bank of the great river, that is, the Tigris, I lifted my eyes and looked, and behold, there was a certain man dressed in linen, whose waist was girded with a belt of pure gold of Uphaz. His body also was like beryl, his face had the appearance of lightning, his eyes were like flaming*

torches, his arms and feet like the gleam of polished bronze, and the sound of his words like the sound of a tumult.

Now I, Daniel, alone saw the vision, while the men who were with me did not see the vision; nevertheless, a great dread fell on them, and they ran away to hide themselves. So I was left alone and saw this great vision; yet no strength was left in me, for my natural color turned to a deathly pallor, and I retained no strength. But I heard the sound of his words; and as soon as I heard the sound of his words, I fell into a deep sleep on my face, with my face to the ground.

Then behold, a hand touched me and set me trembling on my hands and knees. And he said to me, "O Daniel, man of high esteem, understand the words that I am about to tell you and stand upright, for I have now been sent to you." And when he had spoken this word to me, I stood up trembling.

Then he said to me, "Do not be afraid, Daniel, for from the first day that you set your heart on understanding this and on humbling yourself before your God, your words were heard, and I have come in response to your words.

"But the prince of the kingdom of Persia was withstanding me for twenty-one days; then behold, Michael, one of the chief princes, came to help me, for I had been left there with the kings of Persia.

"Now I have come to give you an understanding of what will happen to your people in the latter days, for the vision pertains to the days yet future" (Daniel 10:1-14).

It is clear from this passage that for twenty-one days, the angelic messenger who came to Daniel was detained in some sort of struggle with a demon. Another angel, Michael, was sent to help him. We are not told anything more than that.

We can glean several points from this passage:

- Conflict between angels and demons is occurring in the heavens, **not on earth**.
- While a demon can hinder an angelic messenger from delivering

his word, **the demon eventually loses**.

- This battle that was fought in the heavens involved two angels and one demon but **not** Daniel.

- When the angel needed help against the prince of the kingdom of Persia and God sent another angel to help, God did **not** ask Daniel to pray for more angels; He did **not** give Daniel a sense in his extremely godly prayer life that an angel needed assistance; He did **not** have Daniel identify the demon by name and bind him, so that then—and only then—He could send help.

- God did **not** require Daniel to be involved in any part of the solution in order to have the message delivered. In fact, Daniel didn't even know what was going on until after it was over.

All of these, in some way or another, are exactly what the warfare movement draws from this passage and applies to their method.

What this passage does imply is that Satan has organized his demonic forces to influence kingdoms and nations, and he attempts at every possible point to hinder the Word of God.

Matthew 16:18 states that the gates of hell—that is, the seat of strategy and authority—attempt to prevail against or hinder the Church. However, Christ has already granted victory, not only in the future but the present—**He promised that His Church will not be overtaken**.

Daniel 10 is not a manual for the New Testament believer to begin having prayer walks, binding territorial demons, praying down more angels, or casting out demons from inanimate objects.

Nowhere in God's Word does it say that we are to command demons to give up territory before we can influence neighborhoods, cities, and nations. Nowhere in the Bible does it teach that we are to name demons and bind them in order for the Gospel message to go forward.

I think many people would rather believe that we are to do these things instead of going about the rigors and difficulties of evangelism and discipleship. It is easier to pray for thirty minutes against the demons than it is to study three hours to teach a Sunday School class. It sounds a lot more exciting to walk around the neighborhood casting down the demon of our subdivision than it is to run a Neighborhood Bible Time in our back yard.

Our obedience is to the clear command of Christ, which is **not to go and rebuke demons**, but **to go and make disciples**.

It would be much simpler to pray against the territorial demon of our town and the surrounding towns and then sit back, awaiting the flood of blessings, power, and fruit to roll in. It is another thing altogether to agonize and work in the harvest field week in and week out, where there is a perpetual shortage of laborers.

Christ has told us not to pray for more angels and fewer demons but to pray for more laborers in the harvest field who will invest in the lifelong passion of spiritual reproduction. And while we are at it, our eyes should be upon Jesus Christ, who is the Author and Finisher of our faith.

Could it be that since the enemy of the Church knows he cannot **destroy** us, he spends his time attempting to **distract** us from our true mission?

Kent Hughes, a former pastor of Wheaton College Church, told the story of a couple he knew who had started a Bible study:

The Bible study soon filled their living room with businessmen and women, a couple of doctors, and other professionals. Entire families were being impacted and the Bible study was flourishing.

However, the group began a study on demons, Satan, and the occult. Soon, it so grasped their imagination that they became preoccupied with it. They began to distort Scripture and read authors who wrote of the misapplications of it.

One night, during their Bible study, they dismantled the chandelier in the dining room where they were studying, convinced it was inhabited by a demon. They then took individual pieces of that chandelier to different parts of the city and buried them. The height of embarrassment was when the children of the host family were seen running down the street shouting, "The devil is after us! The devil is after us! . . ." Some neighborhood adults went to the home, wondering what was going on, and found the women in the backyard hacking a rosewood chest with an ax because it, too, was possessed.

Now, one more thing as I finish the introduction to this chapter: living the Christian life victoriously is not for a few experts. It isn't a mystery nor is it obtained by figuring out demonic personalities and incantations for binding the devil. Victory is not for the fortunate Christians who happen to learn how to break through the bondage with a seven-step program.

It may sound far too simplistic and it will not sell many books, but the Bible says:

> **Submit therefore to God. Resist the devil and he will flee from you** (James 4:7).

There are no incantations, no seven steps, no special prayers, no memorized rebukes or bindings, and no dismantled chandeliers and hacked-up chests. The word **resist** is a Greek word that simply means **take a stand against**.

But someone might ask, "How in the world do you resist?" Well, I'm so glad you asked!

In the book of Ephesians, the Spirit of God through the Apostle Paul tells us how to submit to God and how to stand against the devil.

The Author of True Strength

Paul tells us how to be strong against the **snares**, **systems**, and **schemes** of our enemy:

> **Finally, be strong in the Lord and in the strength of His might. Put on the full armor of God, so that you will be able to stand firm against the schemes of the devil** (Ephesians 6:10-11).

Notice that Paul does not say, "Finally, be strong in your **own sense** of confidence and in the strength of your **own spiritual** power."

It's easy to think *I've memorized a chapter of the Bible and I get up early to pray—therefore, I've mastered the basics of Christianity. I'm ready for anything.*

In another letter, Paul writes :

> **[L]et him who thinks he stands take heed that he does not fall** (1 Corinthians 10:12).

Someone might say, "Wait a second—in Ephesians 6, we're told to stand firm, but in 1 Corinthians 10 we're told that when we do stand, we're in trouble. I don't understand the difference!"

The difference is that the believer in 1 Corinthians is standing in his pride and self-sufficiency, while the believer in Ephesians is standing in the power and sufficiency of Christ. One believer is proud of his own spiritual standing and strength, while the other is humbled by his dependence upon the Savior's strength.

The difference between the two believers is remarkable. One thinks that his need of Christ's strength is partial and temporary; the other accepts that his need of Christ's strength is permanent and total.

God said through his prophet:

> *Thus says the LORD, "Let not a wise man boast of his wisdom, and let not the mighty man boast of his might, let not a rich man boast of his riches"* (Jeremiah 9:23).

These are the three things that create a sense of self-sufficiency: **intellectual ability**, **physical health**, and **wealth**.

> *[B]ut let him who boasts boast of this, that he understands and knows Me, that I am the LORD who exercises lovingkindness, justice and righteousness on earth . . .* (Jeremiah 9:24).

The Arena of True Struggle

> *For our struggle is not against flesh and blood, but against the rulers, against the powers, against the world forces of this darkness, against the spiritual forces of wickedness in the heavenly places* (Ephesians 6:12).

What Paul says in this verse is absolutely stunning. He informed the Ephesians that every day they sought to do the will of God, be faithful to Christ, and resist temptation, they were actually engaged in much more—more than temptation or the mundane trials of life. They, as believers, were involved in victorious battle against the powers and personalities of hell.

Paul raised the Christian life to a much higher level. One author wrote,

> *Have you resisted the temptation to be rude toward a colleague? Have you fought off the desire to react with anger against someone who cut you off on the freeway? Have you turned away from a magazine that might have drawn you into lust? Have you restrained your lips from uttering profanity? In doing so, you have struck a blow against the angels of hell in this constant daily battle*[8]

Dear child of God, unless you live with this mentality of war, you are missing out on the drama of life! There is a war going on and you are to relate your life and the events of life to it.

If you haven't gotten to the point where you view life as one divine appointment after another, no matter how trivial or mundane, you are missing out on the taste of victory.

The Armor of True Success

Paul goes on to command the Christian:

Therefore, take up the full armor of God . . . (Ephesians 6:13).

He's literally and emphatically saying, "Put it on!"

By the way, the tense of the verb indicates that we are to put it on once and for all. In other words, this is not a baseball uniform, tennis outfit, or hockey jersey—all of which are removed after the contest. This equipment stays on! Paul says, "Put it on and leave it on—*permanently.*"

Just as our Armed Forces stand on alert and must wear some variation of a Battle Dress Uniform everywhere they go publicly, Paul gets very specific about the pieces of armor.

The Belt of Truth

To understand this concept, you need to erase from your mind the picture of a sash or a belt like one we might wear today. This belt was actually a leather **apron** that was strapped at the waist and went down to just below the thighs. It was the foundational piece of armor. In fact, the breastplate was attached to it and the sword hung from it.

We have discovered already that the battleground of the enemy is on the field of **truth**.

Remember, Satan is called the father of lies in John 8:44 and Paul refers to the deceptive doctrines of demons in 1 Timothy.

Satan counterfeits the truth with his own followers. In Revelation 2:9, we're told about the synagogue of Satan. He has his own ministers and his own false gospel.

All the way back in the Garden of Eden, Satan whispered his gospel into the ear of Eve: "If you disobey God and eat that fruit, you will become one of the gods."

Eve bought it!

In a culture where truth is set aside for whatever you feel you would like to believe, and in the church where doctrine is set aside in favor of experience, how important is the truth of God's Word?

Jesus Christ prayed:

[Father], *"Sanctify them in the* **truth***; Your word is* **truth***"* (John 17:17).

The Apostle John wrote in his second letter:

The elder to the chosen lady and her children, whom I love in **truth***; and not only I, but also all who know the* **truth***, for the sake of the* **truth** *which abides in us and will be with us forever: Grace, mercy and peace will be with us, from God the Father and from Jesus Christ, the Son of the Father, in* **truth** *and love* (2 John 1:1-3).

Now many biblical scholars believe that Paul is not only talking about objective truth—the Word of God—but subjective truth as well: the integrity and honesty that should be a central part of the believer's life.

In our age where nearly eighty percent of people recently polled admitted to some form of dishonesty, the Apostle John writes:

I was very glad to find some of your children walking in **truth** *. . .* (2 John 1:4).

In his third letter, John writes again:

For I was very glad when brethren came and testified to your **truth***, that is, how you are walking in* **truth***. I have no greater joy than this, to hear of my children walking in the* **truth** (3 John 1:3-4).

The believer who truly understands that life is war and the enemy is alive holds to the objective truth of God's Word and walks in honesty and integrity.

In Paul's day, the finest pottery was thin. It had a clear color and brought in a very high price. Fine pottery was very fragile, both before and after firing, and this expensive pottery would often crack in the oven. Cracked pottery should have been thrown away, but there were dishonest dealers who were in the habit of filling in the cracks with a hard pearly wax that would blend in with the color of the pottery. This made the cracks practically disappear, and in the shops, customers would not know—unless they took the pottery outside and held it up to the light. In that case, the cracks would show up darker. Honest dealers often advertised their pottery with a sign that said "sine cera," which meant "without wax." The words "sine cera" (sincere) *became a synonym for* honest *and* integrity, *even to this day.*[9]

Paul says if we want to win the battle—indeed, if we want to stand against the enemy—make sure we strap on the **truth** of the Word and then live it out in trustworthiness, honesty, and sincerity.

Dear reader, there is no excuse for lying, cheating, or deceiving. There is no such thing as a little white lie—if it's a lie, it's sin, and you are missing the central piece of your armor. You are a casualty, not a victor.

In your community, on your campus, or in your business you should be known as a person who tells the truth. If you aren't, do us all a favor and don't tell anyone you're a Christian.

What to Wear to War

Digging Deeper:

How many verses can you find which encourage, teach, exhort, or direct the believer to discover territorial demons and bind them?

Actually, there aren't any! Surprised? What we do have, however, are many verses that give us our mission in life.

And He said to them, "Go into all the world and preach the gospel to all creation" (Mark 16:15).

"Go therefore and make disciples of all the nations, baptizing them in the name of the Father and the Son and the Holy Spirit, teaching them to observe all that I commanded you . . . " (Matthew 28:19-20).

Instead of focusing on a ministry of exorcism, what ministry does God command you to be involved with?

_____

_____

"I also say to you that you are Peter, and upon this rock I will build My church; and the gates of Hades will not overpower it" (Matthew 16:18b).

What does the above verse tell us about the war between the Church and Satan?

_____

_____

_____

Does the believer need to worry which side will win?

Submit therefore to God. Resist the devil and he will flee from you (James 4:7).

There is a very simple truth in this verse: submit to God. **Submit** actually means **to align oneself under the authority of another**. The word for **resist** means **to oppose; to take one's stand against**.

When you surrender to the authority of God and take your stand against the devil, what does this verse promise the devil will do? Casually walk away from you? Come after you with his pitch fork? No way! He's going to *run*!

So what exactly is it that causes Satan to run from you? What could he possibly be so afraid of? Write down some of your thoughts.

_____
_____
_____
_____

What are some ways you can surrender to the authority of God, and resist the devil?

_____
_____
_____
_____

Take It to Heart:

Do you remember the story of young David who stood before Goliath with only five stones and a sling? Even though Goliath was the giant that everyone else in Israel was afraid of, David confidently marched up to him and said these remarkable words:

"You come to me with a sword, a spear, and a javelin, but I come to you in the name of the LORD of hosts, the God of the armies of Israel, whom you have taunted. This day the LORD will deliver you up into my hands, and I will strike you down and remove your head from you. And I will give the dead bodies of the army of the Philistines this day to the birds of the sky and the wild beasts of the earth, that all the earth may know that there is a God in Israel" (1 Samuel 17:45-46).

If you know the rest of the story, you are aware that David slaughtered Goliath. And it wasn't because he had all the modern weaponry or because he was a great marksman with his slingshot; it was because he was fighting in the name of the Lord. God was the One who gave David the victory over his great enemy that day, and it is that same God who offers us victory over our great enemy (the devil) today!

So the question that you need to answer is, "What weapons am I using?"

Paul gives us an entire list of our necessary armor:
Finally, be strong in the Lord and in the strength of His might. Put on the full armor of God, so that you will be able to stand firm against the schemes of the devil (Ephesians 6:10-11).

Read Ephesians 6:14-17. List the weapons/pieces of armor and what each piece provides the believer:

_____

_____

_____

_____

_____

_____

_____

_____

Don't forget prayer!

Don't fight the battle with only five stones and a sling; resist your enemy in the name of the Lord of Hosts . . . and don't forget to wear your armor!

Dressed Up to Kneel Down

The Believer's Safety Net

In the first century when the Apostle Paul lived and preached, the belief in the demonic world was rampant among the Jews. It was largely superstitious and fearful. They believed the air was thickly populated by demons and they could enter a person when they were eating or drinking.

Prior to Paul's day, the Egyptians had already adopted the view that the human body was made of thirty-six parts and a demon could enter and control any one of those parts. It was believed that all illnesses were caused by demons, and they were constantly configuring incantations to exorcise the demons of deafness, dumbness, paralysis, and all sorts of internal aches and pains. There was the common belief in the ancient world that a demon could take away a person's sanity, so the extreme medical practice (or malpractice, to be more accurate) of drilling holes in peoples' skulls was developed. I watched a documentary in which skulls dating back to the time of Christ had been discovered with holes in them.

Even the pagan world intuitively knows of and believes in an unseen world. Tribesmen along the Amazon River today worship evil spirits.

The Bible pulls back the curtain and reveals that unseen world.

Thus far in our study, the Bible has recorded tens of millions of angels worshiping around the throne of God. We have learned that a believer does not have just one angel at work on his behalf but the entire host of angelic beings at the beck and call of God for the believer's well being.

We have seen the highest cherub become the fallen angel of light who led millions of angels to rebel against God and defect from heaven. We have read of Satan's proud intellect and corrupted beauty.

Is the believer helpless? Is it up to us to listen for the whirring of demons' wings? Are we to discover some secret incantation to keep them and their curses from our lives?

We have learned that the believer is safe in Christ. Satan cannot have the soul of a believer; he cannot inhabit a believer; he cannot inhabit objects to bring curses against a believer, for believers are the sanctuary of God.

However, we have been given a warning. Satan has his schemes and snares by which he and his demons attempt to distract the Church and discredit the believer.

The world, the flesh, and the devil are the unholy trinity of evil who war against the trinity of our holy God. They cannot have our soul, as believers, but they can have our testimony. They will gladly have our purity; they will delight in the loss of our integrity and the collapse of our intimacy with Christ. They will welcome our half-hearted worship and service toward the God they hate.

What is the believer to do? Has God left us unprotected? Are we sitting ducks? God's Spirit inhabits us, but is there something for us to do—or are we to stand idly by and hope for the best?

Again, Ephesians 6 answers those questions by commanding believers to dress in a prescribed way with clothing that will protect their mind, their heart, their testimony, and their effective walk with Christ against the lures of the world, the flesh, and the devil.

Dressing for Spiritual Success

The Belt of Truth

Discussed in the last chapter, we begin suiting up for combat by strapping on **the belt of truth**:

Stand firm therefore, having girded your loins with truth . . .
(Ephesians 6:14*a*).

The tense of the verb means you *strap* it on and you *leave* it on.

On the face of the pulpit of our church are the Latin words *Sola Scriptura*, which was the battle cry of the sixteenth century as reformers Calvin, Luther, and Zwingli attempted to reform the corrupted Roman church. Sola Scriptura became their distinctive mantra and means **the Scriptures alone**. Church councils, church fathers, nor church customs determined doctrine and lifestyle. It is the God-inspired Word that should form the basis for faith and practice.

One key result of the Reformation on churches was moving the altar to the side and placing the pulpit in the center of the dais. It was the explanation and declaration that the Scriptures took priority and deserved the most prominent position in the place of corporate worship.

Every Sunday I remind myself that what I have to say is meaningless, and what God has to say is what matters. One of the reasons I've committed my life to teaching through the Bible is that when the Bible is explained, the message I deliver is merely what God has already said. It's the Word of God which is alive and powerful and sharper than any two-edged sword (*Hebrews 4:12*).

I agree with the words of the reformer Martin Luther, who said over four hundred fifty years ago, "The Bible is like a lion; you don't need to defend it, you just need to let it loose."

My passion is to let it loose.

The Christian and the Christian church that holds to Sola Scriptura has strapped around its waist the **belt of truth**. Without it, that believer and church are open and vulnerable to the deceitful doctrines of demons and the snares of Satan.

The Breastplate of Righteousness

Paul tells the believer to:

[P]*ut on the breastplate of righteousness* (Ephesians 6:14*b*).

This righteousness is, first of all, a gift from God through Christ. We call this gift the imputed righteousness of Christ that a believer receives at the moment of salvation.

> *More than that, I count all things to be loss in view of the surpassing value of knowing Christ Jesus my Lord, for whom I have suffered the loss of all things, and count them but rubbish so that I may gain Christ, and may be found in Him, not having a righteousness of my own derived from the Law, but that which is through faith in Christ, the righteousness which comes from God on the basis of faith* (Philippians 3:8-9).

The Roman soldier had a breastplate that covered him from the base of his neck to his upper thighs. It was often made of heavy strips of linen and had pieces of metal or bone sewn or hooked to the linen strips. The wealthier, higher-ranking soldier would have a breastplate made of molded metal. That breastplate covered and protected the heart, in addition to other vital organs.

The believer's heart is covered then, as it were, by the righteousness of Jesus Christ. Our hearts, though deceitful and wicked, have been covered by the blood of Christ.

Now follow this: we are to fight the enemy, not only on the eternal basis of perfected righteousness, but on the daily basis of practical righteousness through obedience. Perfected righteousness comes through Christ; practical righteousness comes through obedience to Christ.

Put differently, as it relates to the breastplate of righteousness, "Spiritual warfare is [literally] an inner struggle [of the heart] for personal holiness."[10]

Solomon wrote:

Watch over your heart with all diligence, for from it flow the springs of life (Proverbs 4:23).

Do you want to know what true spiritual warfare is? It's not binding a demon—it's **resisting temptation**. That is the battle!

When Jesus Christ began His ministry, He didn't go into the wilderness and bind the territorial demon of Jerusalem, nor did He rebuke Satan by the authority of His name—He went out into the wilderness and resisted temptation through the application of Scripture.

The night is almost gone, and the day is near. Therefore let us lay aside the deeds of darkness and put on the armor of light. Let us behave properly as in the day, not in carousing and drunkenness, not in sexual promiscuity and sensuality, not in strife and jealousy. But put on the Lord Jesus Christ, and make no provision for the flesh in regard to its lusts (Romans 13:12-14).

How do you defend yourself in this spiritual warfare? How do you protect yourself? Certainly not by identifying and rebuking demons, but by holy living: relying on the Word; shunning evil; rejecting the excuses that justify sin.

Do you want to enter the battle? **Put on the breastplate of righteousness**; then commit to living a life of holiness as taught in the Word and the onslaught will begin—you will see what spiritual warfare is all about!

The Shoes of Good News

For those of you who will pursue holy living, Paul goes on to say you need a good covering for your feet. He writes,

[A]*nd having shod your feet with the preparation of the gospel of peace* (Ephesians 6:15).

The word **preparation** is the Greek word *etoimasia*, which means **readiness or firmness**.

In other words, "Have your feet laced up with the firm, solid truth of the Gospel of peace."

The Roman soldier's shoes were important—they were considered part of his armor and necessary for at least two things:

1. **Balance** – to provide a solid footing
   In the same way, the Gospel balances us firmly upon the foundation of truth.

   Someone asked a question that I thought was very perceptive: "Since we're supposed to test the spirits, and since Satan is a deceiving angel of light, how will we tell a false teacher or false spirit if they look and sound like the truth?" The answer: False teachers eventually stray from the Gospel—they add something to it or take something away from it. They cannot bear the thought that the Gospel is Christ crucified, buried, and resurrected.

   There are religions that keep Christ on the cross or in Mary's lap as a little baby boy. Some religions make Christ equal with other prophets who have come and gone. But the true Gospel has Christ equal with God—majesty deified, sovereign over all things, and enthroned in His glorified state—not on the cross or in His mother's lap.

   Paul wrote to the Corinthian believers:
   Now I make known to you, brethren, the gospel which I preached to you, which also you received, in which also you stand (1 Corinthians 15:1).

   The Gospel is a pair of shoes that gives you balance as you stand on the truth.

2. **Progress** – to advance
   Roman soldiers had knobs of metal which acted like cleats em-

bedded in their leather soles. They could charge a hill or keep their footing on uneven terrain; they could advance against enemy attacks during hand-to-hand combat.

The soldier did not need cleats if he was retreating. He needed them when climbing, going forward—he needed traction. Like a football player on the gridiron, cleats help him move the ball downfield against opposing forces.

In case you've never noticed, no one wears cleats if they're sitting in the bleachers. I have seen fans wear football helmets, pay one hundred fifty bucks for a jersey, and paint their faces with team colors, but no matter how fanatical or bizarre, I have never seen any fan wearing cleats in the stands—not even once! The field is where the action is. It's where the contest is being waged, and the players are the ones who need the proper shoes for balance and progress.

For the believer in the spiritual battle, Gospel shoes are an imperative.

The Shield of Faith

Paul draws our attention to one of the most fascinating pieces of armor the Romans used in battle. He refers to the shield of faith:

In addition to all, taking up the shield of faith with which you will be able to extinguish all the flaming arrows of the evil one (Ephesians 6:16).

This explicitly states that Satan is an aggressor. He fires flaming arrows, which could be translated "fiery darts; blazing missiles."

Paul, in this verse, is referring to a common practice during his day. When an army came against a city, they tipped their arrows in pitch, lit them, and shot them over the city walls. As soon as those arrows hit the rooftops of buildings, the pitch would splatter and small fires would be started.

There were two kinds of shields in the Roman army. One was a small round shield which was worn on the arm of a soldier in hand-to-hand combat.

The other, called a *thureos* in the Greek, was four feet tall and two feet wide. It was known as the wall. That's the word Paul used in this verse.

This shield was not for hand-to-hand combat. The Roman soldier used it for three different things:

1. **The shield protected the soldier.**
    When Roman soldiers were advancing, there were times that the enemy's flaming arrows came in such a flurry that they would plant their shields into the ground, get behind them, and wait until the attack was over. In the believer's life, there are times when all we can do is plant the shield of faith in God's person, His promises, His providence, and hide behind it.

2. **The shield united the soldiers.**
    The shield literally unified the army. The Roman army had an interesting concept, and it's one of the reasons they were so victorious. The edges of the shields were beveled so they could be locked into place. You could actually have a row of men with shields that made a wall as they advanced against the opposing army.

3. **The shield reflected the sun.**
    The shield was basically made of a large plank of wood. It was overlaid with strips of leather that had been soaked in water. Thus, if a flaming arrow hit it, the water would extinguish the missile. In the center of the shield, a round piece of brass was attached. Before going into battle, the soldier polished that brass so it shone with the brilliance of a mirror. As he walked into battle, the brass piece reflected the light of the sun into the eyes of the enemy and distracted them.

How wonderful that, **with this shield of faith, we can reflect the light of God's Son**, the Light of the world. It can shine into the world around us—into the eyes, so to speak, of our enemy.

The Helmet of Salvation

Paul continues:

And take the helmet of salvation . . . (Ephesians 6:17*a*).

Now, this does not refer to being saved. Paul is not saying that after you put on the shoes, the belt, and the breastplate, you now get saved. That cannot be what he is talking about, because you wouldn't have that armor if you weren't saved. In fact, you would not be in the army as a soldier of Christ if you were not saved.

A soldier's helmet protected his head—his mind, his thoughts. Salvation is that propositional truth that we believe. There are three parts to salvation:

1. **Justification** - **past** work of salvation; has been accomplished

    You were saved when Christ called you to Himself, when you received that gift of eternal life. You were saved and you never need to doubt it. It is accomplished and finished.

2. **Sanctification** - **present** work of salvation; continuous

    Surprisingly, for every ten people who doubt the past work of justification to be complete, there are a thousand believers who doubt the fact that God is working continuously in their lives right now (sanctification).

3. **Glorification** - **future** salvation; **absolutely guaranteed!**

Herein we find the three-fold work of salvation. **Put on this helmet of the truth of salvation to protect your mind.**

The Sword of the Spirit

Finally, Paul says,
And take . . . the sword of the Spirit, which is the word of God (Ephesians 6:17*b*).

The text tells us that we have an offensive weapon. It is not our ingenuity or resourcefulness, incantations, bindings, or rebukes. **It is the Word of God.**

When Jesus Christ went into the wilderness to be tempted, He didn't cast anyone down or bind the devil. He was tempted three times and all three times, the first words out of His mouth were, "It is written . . . " He encountered the enemy and used the sword of the Spirit, which is the Word of God.

Now, the Roman sword was two feet long. It had sharpened sides and was pointed at the end. The writer of Hebrews refers to this:

> **[T]***he word of God is . . . sharper than any two-edged sword . . .* (Hebrews 4:12).

That writer was thinking of the nuclear bomb of ancient warfare! It was the most powerful weapon known. He said **God's Word is sharper than any two-edged sword.**

The sword is the only piece of armor that is offensive and comes in contact with the enemy. Remember, it is the one thing that gives us the assurance that we can advance against our enemy. And Paul says,

[T]*he sword of the Spirit, which is the word of God* (Ephesians 6:17*b*).

Do you remember when Jesus Christ was tempted? He responded three ways; what did He say?

It is written . . . (Matthew 4).

When my twin sons were around six years old, we were at the airport to pick up my mother-in-law, who was coming to spend the holidays with us. As we were waiting, soldiers dressed in fatigues disembarked from the same plane that she was on. They were an incredible sight, wearing their BDUs and having their guns strapped to their sides. These men filed past us as we were standing right by the door (this was pre-9/11), and my boys were awestruck. They stood there watching the soldiers, and one of my sons said, "Dad, there's those army men." A soldier stopped, looked down at him, and said, "Boy, we're not Army—we're **Marines.**" *I was tempted to say, "I don't know whose kid this is . . . go find your parents, son."*

Those men were prepared for battle. But imagine what it would be like if they had well-armored tanks, the fastest planes, and the latest weapons but nothing was loaded! There were no bullets or bombs. That would make them just a defensive force. And no matter how capable, the best defensive force will eventually break down unless there is advancement—ground gained.

The same is true of the Christian army. Paul is implying that the army of Jesus Christ is advancing . . . gaining ground. We have an offensive strategy and weaponry to achieve it.

What is it? **[T]*he sword of the Spirit, which is the word of God*** (Ephesians 6:17*b*).

Dressed Up to Kneel Down . . . and Pray

Having covered all of this ground with the believer, Paul says that we are, in effect, all dressed up for war. So, what do we do now?

***With all prayer and petition pray at all times in the Spirit,
and with this in view, be on the alert with all perseverance and
petition for all the saints*** (Ephesians 6:18).

Just imagine a soldier getting dressed in his armor, going out onto the battlefield, and kneeling to pray.

Why should we pray?

- **We're going to fight things we cannot see by ourselves.**
- **We're going to fight things we cannot defeat by ourselves.**

Paul says it's possible to fight the battle without the right armor. The truth is, it's possible to be a believer and not have the full armor of God. But he says to the believer, "Take it up! Put it on!"

And after that admonition, Paul tells us, "On your mark, get set, *kneel.* That's right, soldiers: get dressed up *to pray!*"

Dear reader, the battle is won or lost in private before it is ever fought in public.

No Christian is exempt from danger—temptation is the enemy of every one of us.

It is possible to face Satan and his attacks ill-equipped and, therefore, not be able to resist. God intends the sword to swing and the Church to advance. It will only be done by people who will put on the armor and bow their knee to the One who gives victory.

In one of his books, Gary Richmond tells the story of a young zoo-keeper named Julie :

The zoo had purchased a baby raccoon and it was among Julie's duties to care for him. Playful, cuddly, puppy-like in its antics, it soon won Julie's heart, as well as the hearts of everyone else in that section of the zoo. Julie could often be seen doing her duties with her cute little raccoon perched on her shoulder. She even named him Bandit.

Gary's experience, however, caused him to worry for Julie. He told her that raccoons go through a glandular change at about twenty-four months of age. After that, they will often, inexplicably, viciously attack their owners. A thirty-pound raccoon can do the same kind of damage as a large dog. Over and over again, Gary warned his young friend about her growing pet. She would always listen politely as he explained the coming danger.

Richmond wrote, "I will never forget her answer; it was always the same: 'It will be different for me,' she would say with a smile, as she added, 'Bandit wouldn't hurt me. He just wouldn't.'"

Then Richmond wrote, "Three months after my last warning, Julie underwent plastic surgery for severe facial lacerations sustained when her adult raccoon attacked her for no apparent reason. Bandit was released into the wild."

Sin too often comes dressed in an enticing guise. And as we become entangled in it, it's easy to say, "It will be different for me."

When the Lord taught His disciples to pray, that prayer included the words,

[D]*eliver us from evil . . .* (Matthew 6:13*a*).

In other words, "Lord, I can handle anything but temptation, and I will admit that. I will get into trouble if left to myself: I'll adopt some sin and say it really won't hurt me; I'll justify compromise and say it's all right for me. Lord, I am admitting that I can't take care of myself. Please protect me from the tempter."

The Church at large has gone off on a journey into a warfare that lacks biblical justification. It is binding, rebuking, laying hold of, and sending to the abyss of hell all sorts of demonic beings. That only reveals a lack of spiritual understanding, according to Jude 10 and 2 Peter 2:12.

And what has happened to the Church? It's more immoral, indistinct, confused, and ineffective than ever before. The Church has become distracted by the enemy.

Dear friend, true spiritual warfare is that daily battle for purity, integrity, compassion, holiness, spiritual fruit, character, and love. You are going to fight it every day, every hour, every minute.

Take Paul's advice: get dressed up and kneel down—pray for God's Spirit to completely dominate your thinking and your actions; pray that His Word will fill you and flow through you.

This is what it means to live with your armor on. This is what James meant when he said :

Submit therefore to God. Resist the devil and he will flee from you (James 4:7).

So strap on your armor, grab your sword and shield, advance against the enemy, and *pray . . . pray . . . PRAY*!

Dressed Up to Kneel Down

Digging Deeper:

The three components of the holy triune God are: the Father, the Son and the Holy Spirit. According to our current study, what three things make up the unholy trinity of evil?

1._____

2._____

3._____

Paul wrote:

Stand firm therefore, having girded your loins with truth (Ephesians 6:14).

The original term for gird your loins can also be rendered gird your waist. In the context of apparel, the words refer to covering up or hiding. How can you cover your waist/body with truth? And why would this be an important action for the believer?

_____

_____

_____

_____

_____

Watch over your heart with all diligence, for from it flow the springs of life (Proverbs 4:23).

The phrase "watch over your heart" can also be translated to say "guard your heart." In Psalm 15:1-2, David says that the only person who may have communion with God is the one who has clean hands and a pure heart.

What are some areas in your life where you haven't been completely guarding your heart or you haven't been very diligent in keeping your actions pure?

Reading material? TV? Conversation? Movies? Relationships?

_____

_____

_____

_____

After you have identified the areas in your heart that still need covering/guarding, ask the Lord right now to give you diligence and fresh discipline. Write out below three resolutions to strengthen your heart and mind.

Resolution #1

_____
_____

Resolution #2

_____
_____

Resolution #3

_____
_____

And take . . . the sword of the Spirit, which is the word of God. With all prayer and petition pray at all times in the Spirit . . . (Ephesians 6:17*b*-18*a*).

According to this verse, what is our **offensive** weapon in this battle for purity, integrity, and spiritual victory?

_____
_____

Read Luke 4:1-13 and notice how Christ Himself used this weapon to show us how to overcome temptation. Each of Satan's temptations was met with a verse of Scripture from the same Old Testament Book.

Temptation #1 (turn stones into bread)
Christ's defense: _____

Temptation #2 (worship me [the devil])
Christ's defense: _____

Temptation #3 (throw Yourself down, testing Your power and the protection of the Father)
Christ's defense: _____

Take It to Heart:

"[D]eliver us from evil" (Matthew 6:13*a*).

Let's be perfectly honest . . . we all have personal struggles and are often tempted to give in to sin on a daily basis. While everyone's temptation is different to some degree from others, many times we as Christians will allow ourselves to use those struggles as a license to sin. Our problem is **not** that we don't have the strength or the means to overcome temptation. God has given us everything we need for life and godliness! Our problem is that we don't have the desire to overcome temptation.

You and I need to stop praying for strength when we are tempted because we already have strength. Rather, we need to pray for the **desire** to resist temptation and keep our hearts pure. That is what we most lack today—desire.

Ask yourself these questions:
- What am I having a hard time getting rid of in my life?
- Are there certain temptations that I am more vulnerable to?
- If temptation were to keep persisting in my life, when am I most vulnerable?

Search your own heart and then write down two areas of temptation in your life where you seem to be lacking the desire to change.

1._____
_____

2._____
_____

Don't forget this! Identifying your area of struggle is only the **first step** to personal holiness. The next step is to pray that God will give you the desire to overcome this temptation today. He can and He will!

Paul encourages the Christian with these words:

Not that I have already obtained it or have already become perfect, but I press on so that I may lay hold of that for which also I was laid hold of by Christ Jesus. Brethren, I do not regard myself as having laid hold of it yet; but one thing I do: forgetting what lies behind and reaching forward to what lies ahead, I press on toward the goal for the prize of the upward call of God in Christ Jesus (Philippians 3:12-14).

In other words . . . **don't ever give up!**

ENDNOTES

1   Duane A. Garrett, *Angels and the New Spirituality* (Nashville, TN, Broadman and Holman, 1995), chapter 5.

2   Larry Richards, *Every Good and Evil Angel in the Bible* (Nashville, TN, Thomas Nelson Publishers, 1998), p. 173.

3   John MacArthur, *How to Meet the Enemy* (Victor Publishing, 1992), p. 7.

4   David Jeremiah, *What the Bible Says about Angels* (Walk Through The Bible Publishers, 1995), p. 58.

5   MacArthur, *How to Meet the Enemy*, p. 23.

6   Jeremiah, *What the Bible Says about Angels*, p. 73.

7   Donald G. Mostrom, *Intimacy with God* (Tyndale House Publishers, 1984).

8   Garrett, *Angels and the New Spirituality*, p. 228.

9   MacArthur, *How to Meet the Enemy*, p. 85.

10 MacArthur, *How to Meet the Enemy*, p. 95.

Scripture Index